Robert Schumann

SCHUMANN
his life and times

SCHUMANN
his life and times

Tim Dowley

Robert Schumann, by
Bendemann

Paganiniana Publications

ISBN 0-87666-634-9

For my Mother

Published by PAGANINIANA PUBLICATIONS, INC.
211 West Sylvania Avenue
Neptune City, New Jersey 07753

Contents

Acknowledgements

Illustrations reproduced by kind permission of
The Mansell Collection, Radio Times Hulton
Picture Library and the Mary Evans Picture
Library.

Robert Schumann

Schumann's birthplace in Zwichau

1 A Zwickau Childhood

Robert Alexander Schumann was born in the small riverside town of Zwickau, Saxony, in 1810. The local paper, the *Zwickauer Wochenblatt*, announced:

On 8 June to Herr August Schumann, notable citizen and bookseller here, a little son.

The son of a clergyman, August Schumann was born in 1773, and did not become a 'notable citizen' without great effort. His early life was an uphill struggle against poverty and his parents' opposition. Poor himself, August's father tried to steer his son into a safe, solid career. But August was irresistibly drawn to poetry, and even sent some of his early efforts to the bookseller Heinse for criticism. Heinse was not terribly impressed, but in 1792 August Schumann, now working as a grocer's assistant in Leipzig, enrolled

Robert Schumann's home
in Zwickau

as an arts student at the city's university. There he remained until money ran out. Driven back penniless to his father's house, he began work on a novel, *Knightly Scenes and Monkish Tales*, and although Heinse was again non-committal about its literary merits, the bookseller did offer August a job, as assistant in his shop at Zeitz.

August accepted, and all went well until he fell for Johanna Schnabel, the daughter of his landlord, who was the municipal surgeon. Objections to their match were strong, and an engagement was allowed only after Schumann agreed to give up bookselling for the more lucrative trade of grocery.

With his predilection for literature, over the next eighteen months August published several books, including novels and a commercial handbook, *The Merchants' Companion*, and scraped together 1000 thaler to buy a shop. In 1799 August was able to turn once more to bookselling, opening his own shop in Zeitz. In 1808 he moved to the small town of Zwickau on the river Mulde, where, partnered by one of his brothers, he ran a prosperous business from a shop in the main square.

August does not seem to have been particularly musical, but his literary drive was strong, and he published many novels and stories. However his commercial and statistical works were more readily received by the reading public. He also launched a series of successful pocket editions of the classics of 'all the nations', and translated Byron's *Beppo* and *Childe Harold* into German.

Occasionally August's restlessness and anxiety threatened his stability, and he verged on nervous breakdown. He suffered particularly severely during the year of Robert's birth.

Of Robert's mother Johanna we have a much vaguer picture. One writer claimed that in later life:

She fell into an exaggerated state of romance and sentimentalism, together with sudden, violent passion, and a tendency to eccentricity, to which marital differences may have contributed.

She is also described as pedantic, unimaginative and intensely morbid. Unfortunately Robert seems to have inherited something of both his parents' neurotic characteristics.

The youngest of five children, Robert Schumann was brought up in comfortable, middle-class respectability. As a child, he apparently exhibited no particularly remarkable abilities, and the Schumanns' home life was generally secure and peaceful. Possibly, as the youngest of five, Robert was rather spoiled.

In 1812, Europe was still blasted by war. Napoleon raised a great army of half-a-million men, and marched east towards Russia. His route lay through the little town of Zwickau, which found itself

Robert Schumann

traversed by columns of marching soldiers and platoons of cavalry, who took two days to pass through. The following year, during the disastrous retreat from Moscow, their route again brought them through Zwickau. Starving soldiers looted for food, and brought disease and plague. The wounded filled the town's hospitals, unhygenic conditions encouraged the spread of cholera, and nearly five hundred citizens of Zwickau died in a matter of weeks. Such devastation inevitably marked the Schumann family, and particularly the impressionable children.

At the age of six, Robert was sent to the local preparatory school, run by Archdeacon Döhner. He had in fact already begun his education, with the young tutor who gave lessons in exchange for board and lodging at the Schumann home.

At the age of seven Robert received his first piano lessons, from Johann Gottfried Kuntzsch, organist at St Mary's Church, and schoolmaster at the Zwickau Lyceum. Kuntzsch was a kindly, conservative musician of limited abilities; his knowledge stemmed from leisure-time study. Despite his persistent attempts to drum up musical interest in Zwickau by joint performances by the choir, orchestra and military band, Kuntzsch's musical gifts were not great. Nevertheless, Robert was soon improvising, and even composing a set of dances for the piano. A friend remembered:

He could sketch the personalities of his friends by figures and passages on the piano, so that everyone burst into laughter at the accuracy of the portrait.

Schumann did not forget Kuntzsch's help. In 1832, in a letter accompanying a laurel-wreath to mark the fiftieth anniversary of Kuntzsch's appointment as teacher at the Lyceum, Robert said:

You were the only one who recognised my musical talent and pointed me to the path along which sooner or later my good genius would guide me.

Robert's musical talent was also recognised by his father. He bought an expensive Streicher grand piano for his son, and soon four-handed arrangements of the classics were heard in the Schumann home. With a friend named Friedrich Piltzing, another pupil of Kuntzsch's, Robert started to explore Haydn, Mozart and Beethoven. He also occasionally played his own pieces, to the delight of his father, August. His most ambitious work seems to have been a setting of Psalm 150 for voices and instrumental accompaniment.

As a child, Schumann took part in several concerts at the Zwickau Lyceum. He once played Moscheles' *Alexander March* variations, which demanded considerable dexterity. In the summer of 1819,

Ignaz Moscheles
composer and pianist;
1794-1870

11

Carlsbad

Robert went to hear the great Ignaz Moscheles play at Carlsbad. This experience left an indelible impression: in 1851 he wrote to Moscheles that he still preserved as a 'sacred relic' a concert programme that the pianist had held in his hands more than thirty years earlier. At about this time too Robert attended his first opera when August Schumann organised a trip to Leipzig to hear Mozart's *Magic Flute*. But already Robert's main enthusiasm was for the piano.

Meanwhile Kuntzsch continued to encourage Robert's musical interest. In November 1821, Robert played the piano at a performance at St Mary's Church of a long-since forgotten oratorio by Friedrich Schneider, *Weltgericht*.

On one occasion the score and orchestra parts for the overture to Righini's opera *Tigrama* were delivered by mistake to the Schumann bookshop. Robert collected together his musical friends and acquaintances to make up a band of two flutes, violins and horns, and a single clarinet, and directed the performance, while filling in at the piano.

At the Lyceum Robert was active as both pianist and public speaker. When he was fourteen, Kuntzsch decided that his pupil had progressed beyond the point where he could give further help, and declined to teach him any longer.

Since his early years, Robert had spent hours browsing among his father's books. As a result, his reading tastes developed freely, and at the age of thirteen he compiled his own anthology of verse, which included some of his own poetry. In 1828 he made a second collection, this time almost wholly composed of his own verse, and strongly influenced by the contemporary fashion for metrical versions of Latin poetry. Meanwhile in a notebook Robert wrote down his own translation of several of Horace's Odes, which were so admired by Beethoven.

Shortly before leaving the Lyceum, Schumann collaborated with his brother Karl in preparing a new edition of Forcellini's Latin dictionary, *Lexicon Totius Latinitatis*. Perhaps August harboured secret hopes that his youngest son would embark on a literary career.

While still at the Lyceum, Robert's fondness for societies and clubs began to show itself. About 1825 he took a leading part in founding two: the secret Schülverbindung, devoted to fencing and gymnastics, and soon afterwards a literary society, called the Schülverein, which took as its maxim:

It is the duty of every cultivated man to know his country's literature.

Robert's letters to Emil Flechsig, a friend at Leipzig University, throw further light on his literary tastes. He loved Caesar, Cicero, Homer, Horace, Plato, Sophocles and Tacitus, and of contemporary German writers admired Schiller. But Robert stated that Goethe as yet lay beyond his understanding. Already it was romantic literature which most fired his imagination. Robert's idol and model was the sentimental novelist 'Jean Paul' (JP Richter). Many of his letters contain extravagant praise for this passionate writer, and are written in close imitation of his style. For example Schumann wrote to Flechsig in 1827:

All those joyful hours which I spent with you, my old friend, came

Jean Paul Friedrich
Richter

thronging before my soul, and with a saddened spirit I went forth to be
with Nature, and I read your letter, read it ten times over; while a last kiss
from glowing lips was touching the sweetly fading green of the wooded
heights; golden cloudlets floated in the pure aether . . .

One of the greatest joys of his last days at school was to visit the
home of Karl Carus, a Zwickau merchant and music-lover. Years
later Robert described the atmosphere in the Carus household as
'joy, serenity and music'. It was in their home that 'the names
Mozart, Haydn and Beethoven were among those talked of daily
with enthusiasm . . . In his home I first got to know the later works
of these masters'.

It was there, too, that Robert met Agnes Carus, wife of Dr
Eduard Carus, Karl's nephew. Young, pretty and intelligent, and a
gifted singer, Agnes attracted Robert, who was soon writing songs
for her and accompanying her in Schubert *lieder* at parties at their
home at Colditz, just outside Zwickau.

14

Schubert making music
with friends

Robert was awakening to the attractions of the opposite sex. He fell for a young woman called Liddy Hempel, and at the same time became infatuated with Nanni Patsch, of whom he wrote, in imitation of Jean Paul:

O friend! Were I but a smile, how I would flit about her eyes! Were I but joy, how gently would I throb in all her pulses! Yea, might I be but a tear, I would weep with her, and then if she smiled again, how gladly would I die on her eyelash, and gladly be no more!

Robert soon subsided into 'pure, divine friendship and reverence . . . like devotion to the madonna', and consoled himself by writing an autobiographical story, *Juniusabende und Juliatage* – a piece he described two years later as 'my first work, my truest and my finest; how I wept as I wrote it and yet how happy I was!' But his double-affair with Liddy and Nanni was quite an achievement for provincial Zwickau.

In 1826, Emilie, Robert's nineteen-year-old sister, killed herself. She had contracted a skin disease, which in its turn precipitated severe depression. During an attack of typhus, she left the house and drowned herself. Her father August never recovered from this blow. A few weeks later he himself died, while his wife Johanna was away at Carlsbad. Robert was permanently scarred by these deaths. He developed an obsessive fear of death and funerals, and could not bear the ordeal of attending his mother's funeral in 1836.

August left his fortune to his family, and Robert inherited 8000 thaler. A guardian, Gottlob Rudel, was appointed to help administer the money. Rudel, a cloth and iron merchant in Zwickau, was 'a stiff businessman who looked as if he had swallowed a ruler'.

But life for Robert was not entirely gloomy. He wrote to his friend Flechsig of excursions into the countryside, and as far as Dresden, Teplitz and Prague. At Teplitz, a prominent spa, he once more met – and parted with – Liddy Hempel. This occasioned one of Robert's purplest pieces of prose, in imitation of Jean Paul:

The whole of flowering nature stretched before me: to the east a succession of cloudy blue mountains rose up on the horizon; the temple of all nature opened wide and deep before my intoxicated eyes. I should have liked to fly away and plunge into those torrents of flowers . . . Would you too not have been tempted to forget yourself and admit that the world is beautiful? The sun had vanished at last, shafts of brilliant pink shot from its dying rays; the mountains glowed, the forests blazed, and inexhaustible creation scattered itself in masses of roses. Looking at the purple ocean, all I saw contracted to one single idea. Divine thoughts uplifted me: God, nature and the beloved one stood before me, smiling kindly, when all at once a dark cloud rose in the east, from which came a flash of lightning, and other

Carl Maria von Weber

16

Carl Maria von Weber

Efter C. Hornemans Tegning.

Af Originalpartituren til „Freischütz".

17

clouds piled high in the sky. Then I seized Liddy's hand and said 'Look, Liddy, at the image of life'. I showed her the dark purple on the horizon. She looked at me sadly, a tear ran down her cheek.

. . . Silently I picked a rose and was about to give it to her when thunder and lightning set fire to the east. I took the rose and tore off the petals. The thunder clap had awoken me from my sweet dream. I was once more down to earth. Liddy sat before me, tears welling up in her blue eyes. She studied the wild mass of clouds. 'Look, that is our life', I might have said to her. We left . . . without speaking a word. When I said goodbye to her she squeezed my hand; the dream was over. And the sublime image of the ideal faded away when I thought of the things she had said about Jean Paul.

A lively letter to Flechsig recalls the climax to a winter tour when, after dining at a country inn, Schumann and his party entertained the peasants with singing, stories and dances:

We whirled the peasant girls about in tremendous style. I danced with gentle, modest Minchin of the Müllers, while Walther pretended to play. Old Müller and his wife joined in the dance, the rustics stamped their feet. We rejoiced and rushed about, staggering among the legs of the clodhoppers, and then took a tender farewell of the whole company by smacking kisses on the lips of all the peasant girls, Minchin and the rest.

The same year, 1827, the seventeen-year-old Robert Schumann started to keep a diary, which is full of revealing entries. There were, for instance, 'daily improvisations' and 'beginnings of a piano concerto in F minor'.

Sensing his son's talent, August Schumann had considered sending Robert to study with Weber, the composer of the opera *Der Freischütz*. But now Robert had to consider a very different future. Like her father-in-law, Johanna Schumann believed the arts offered little prospect of either security or success. On 15 March 1828, after Robert had graduated from the Lyceum, he was sent by his mother and his guardian to the University of Leipzig to study law. In fact he had not the slightest intention of pursuing law, but went to Leipzig the better to be able to cajole, coax, persuade and coerce Johanna to alter her plans.

2 Student Years

Market-place and town-hall, Leipzig

'School is now behind my back and the world lies ahead. As I went out of school for the last time, I could scarcely keep back my tears; but the joy was still stronger than the pain. Now the true inner man must come forward and show who he is.' Despite his distaste for law and the absence of family and friends, Robert was at first inclined to make an adventure of student days in Leipzig.

Robert Schumann

Here I am, without guide, teacher or father, flung helplessly into the darkness of life's unknown, and yet the world has never seemed fairer than at this moment, as I cheerfully face its storms. Flechsig, you must stand by me, my friend, in the whirl of life, and help me if I fail.

20

In his notebook for Easter 1828 Robert noted:

Night raptures. Constant improvisation daily. Also literary fantasies in Jean Paul manner. Special enthusiasm for Schubert, Beethoven too, Bach less. Letter to Franz Schubert (not sent).

Before setting out for Leipzig, Robert had to make arrangements about his lodgings. When Flechsig and his friend Moritz Semmel, a law student and brother of Robert's sister-in-law, offered Robert rooms in their lodgings, he was happy to accept.

Flechsig and Semmel took their companion in hand, showing him new sights and faces. Semmel introduced Robert to Gisbert Rosen, a Jewish law student in his final year at Heidelberg University.

Heinrich Heine

Their friendship was strengthened by a mutual admiration for Jean Paul, and Robert immediately invited his new friend home to Zwickau, where they stayed for a fortnight, enjoying the wedding festivities of Robert's brother, Julius.

Then the two young men set off to explore Bavaria, with its mountains, forests and medieval castles. Schumann accompanied Rosen as far as Munich on his erratic journey to Heidelberg. Travelling by stage-coach, their first stop was Bayreuth, one-time home of Jean Paul. They managed to extract from his widow a portrait of their idol, and spent hours searching out his local haunts. They then went on to Augsburg, staying for a few nights with Dr Kurrer, a chemist, and August Schumann's closest friend. The doctor had an attractive daughter, Clara, in whom Robert became interested; only letters of introduction to the poet Heinrich Heine in Munich tempted him away again. Now thirty-one, Heine greeted his young admirers coolly – meeting them at home, and a second time at the Leuchtenberg Gallery.

Schumann and Rosen eventually parted at Munich. For Robert, the farewell was emotional, and he lapsed into his habitual melancholia. He wrote to Rosen from Leipzig:

My journey through Augsburg was confoundedly dull, and I missed you terribly in those ultra Catholic regions. I never care to describe my travels, let alone when they arouse unpleasant feelings, which are better erased from our memories. I will say only that I thought of you most affectionately, that both sleeping and waking sweet Clara's image was always in front of my eyes, and that I was heartily glad to see my dear native Zwickau once again.

But he stayed in Zwickau only long enough to pack his bags and travelled on to Leipzig weeping bitterly.

Life in Leipzig, a busy market-town criss-crossed with alleys and streets converging on the market square, confused Robert. He wanted to be back in provincial Zwickau, and his first letters home complain of homesickness, loneliness and a yearning to leave the city and return to the fields and open-air of his native Zwickau.

It is hard to find nature here. Everything is ornamented by art. There is no valley, no mountain, no wood, where I can totally lose myself in my thoughts, no spot where I can be alone, unless it's locked up in my room, with everlasting noisy uproar going on below.

On another occasion, slipping back into Jean Paul's idiom, he wrote:

Alas, why do we appreciate happiness only after it has left us, and why does each tear one sheds contain either a dead pleasure or a vanished blessing?

Once more he gave way to self-pity. But in an unguarded moment he was truthful enough to describe his lodgings as excellent, and friends later confirmed that his rooms were better than the average student's.

Robert's friends, the Caruses, had just settled in Leipzig, Dr Carus having been appointed Professor of Medicine at the University. In the friendly atmosphere of their home, Robert accompanied Agnes, and played chamber music. He also made a number of useful and interesting contacts, among them the composer Wolfgang Marschner and the piano teacher Friedrich

Friedrich Wieck

Wieck. At a musical party, Wieck's precocious nine-year-old daughter Clara played the piano for a trio by Hummel 'amazingly well'. Robert coolly noted that her nose was too long, and her eyes too big! But he also arranged to take piano lessons with her father.

Limited though Robert's circle of friends was, many student societies were open to him, catering for debating, fencing, athletics, smoking and drinking, among other activities. Financially, too, he was well looked after, his mother frequently mailing parcels from home, and even promising him expensive riding lessons.

The main problem lay with Robert's morose, introspective temperament. He was uneasy and unsure of himself in company and frequently admitted that, among people who did not understand him, and for whom he could raise little interest, he felt miserable.

For his fellow students, with their ideas about a new Germany and nationalism, he had contempt; but he took a liking to Götte, a strong-minded philology student with whom he corresponded in the vacation. Flechsig and Semmel remained Robert's closest friends, although he wrote to his mother that Flechsig 'never cheers me up! If I am depressed he ought not to be so too, and might be decent enough to brighten me up.'

But Robert made few intimate friends. There was also the problem of his lack of interest in law. Even his first letter home had an unpromising end:

I am perplexed beyond measure by the choice of study. Chilly jurisprudence, with its ice-cold definitions, would crush the life out of me from the outset. Medicine I will not, theology I cannot, study. So–I struggle endlessly with myself, and look in vain for someone to tell me what to do. But there is nothing to be done. I must choose law.

Although Flechsig later suggested that Robert did not in fact attend a single lecture, he does seem to have shown an initial flicker of interest in it. Letters to his mother mention that he is only making notes 'mechanically', but attending lectures 'regularly'. To his guardian Rudel, Robert wrote: 'I certainly decided on law as my profession, and shall work hard at it, however dry and uninteresting it may be at the start'.

However on 14 August 1828 Robert wrote to his friend Rosen that he had not yet attended any lectures. It is unclear where the truth lay–though his inclinations are evident. According to Flechsig, Schumann spent his days writing imitations of Jean Paul. His *Hottentottiana* featured Robert in the guise of the hero, Gustav, in an autobiographical novel. He also wrote bits and pieces of short stories, and some notes for a study of musical aesthetics.

As soon as he arrived in Leipzig, Robert fixed himself up with a piano and improvised whenever he could. Turning for inspiration to lyric poetry, he completed settings of Goethe's ballad *Der Fischer* and three poems by Justius Kerner. These, with earlier songs, he sent to Gottlob Wiedebein, musical director at Brunswick, for an opinion. Wiedebein replied:

Your songs have many, sometimes very many, shortcomings; but I should call them sins not so much of the spirit as of nature and youth, and these are excusable and pardonable where pure poetic feeling and genuine spirit shines through. And it is precisely that which has pleased me so much.

Confessing that he was 'purely and simply guided by nature', and would set about studying composition, Robert responded:

Live as happily as you deserve to; for you have given many happy moments to many people and to me my happiest.

Shortly after this Robert wrote to his mother:

A nineteenth-century string quarter

In my own heart I am not quite so joyless, and what my fellow creatures cannot give me is given me by music. My piano tells me all the deep sentiments which I cannot express.

VIEUXTEMPS.   DELOFFRE.   HILL.   PIATTI.   ELLA.

25

Frankfurt

Meanwhile the piano lessons with Wieck were proceeding. Difficult as Robert found it to adapt to Wieck's 'quiet, cold, well-considered, restrained conquest of technique', he gained much from his lessons. Many hours were spent at Wieck's house, often in the company of nine-year-old Clara.

Robert was also gradually emerging from his shell. Among his fellow students he discovered a violinist, Täglichsback, and a cellist, Glock. With Schumann at the piano, a cigar between his lips, the three would make music late into the night. On occasion they were joined by Sörgel, a viola player, and Wieck would come to listen to their performances.

Such activities soon stimulated Robert to compose. He now completed a piano quartet in C minor and a set of eight polonaises for piano duet, all written for these musical evenings at his lodgings. Franz Schubert was his current idol; when in November 1828 Robert heard that Schubert had died, Flechsig heard him sobbing with grief into the night. Later Schumann wrote that

Schubert's name 'should only be whispered at night to the trees and the stars'.

With the autumn there was also the new season of concerts at Leipzig's *Gewandhaus* to attend. Schumann was forward enough to suggest that next season he would play a four-handed concerto with Mlle Reichold, one of Leipzig's best virtuosos.

But Robert was all the time pining for his friend Rosen, and for Heidelberg. There now occurred a good pretext to go there; a professor of law, Justus Thibaut, who had also written on musical aesthetics, was now lecturing at Heidelberg. In 1829 Robert wrote to his mother and his guardian pleading to be allowed to change universities. They agreed, and on 11 May 1829 Robert set out for his new home. En route he found himself travelling to Frankfurt with the young best-selling novelist Willibald Alexis. As a result, Robert did not go direct from Frankfurt to Heidelberg, but went off to Coblenz, sailing from Bingen through the beautiful Rheingau, and ended up penniless at the end of the trip.

In the Rhineland Robert let himself go, revelling in the eccentricities of his travelling companions. At Frankfurt he visited a music shop, announcing that he was tutor to an English aristocrat who was looking for a good piano. After three hours' solid practice, during which he was much 'stared at and applauded', Robert promised to let the shopkeeper know his employer's decision in a day or two. By that time, Robert was far away in Rüdesheim, drinking Rüdesheimer.

A letter to his mother recounts some of his adventures, but without the gross sentimentality of his previous effforts. Eventually he arrived in Heidelberg:

And yet, my bright little Heidelberg, you are so lovely, so innocent and idyllic. If one may compare the Rhine and its rocky hills with a fine strong man, so the Neckar valley might be compared with a beautiful woman. There, all is massive and rugged, vibrating with old Teutonic harmonies; here everything breathes a soft melodious song of Provence.

Robert knew he would eventually have to return to Leipzig to take his degree, but made his time in Heidelberg as enjoyable as he could. He wrote home in July:

I'm industrious and regular, and enjoying my jurisprudence under Thibaut and Mittermayer enormously. Only now am I beginning to realise its real value, and the way it helps all the loftiest interests of humanity. Good heavens, what a contrast there is between the Leipzig professor who stood there like a mechanical toy climbing up the Jacob's-ladder of automatic promotion, rattling off his paragraphs without any form of eloquence or inspiration, and Thibaut, who, though twice his age, is

27

A quarter of Frankfurt

overflowing with life and ideas, and can hardly find word or time to express his feelings!

Robert noticed that the standard of musical performance was lower than in Leipzig, and that his own playing was regarded as exceptional. But he was as interested in the cost of living in the town, in the women he met, and in 'the scores of other acquaintances to whom I bow in the street and with whom I exchange small talk'.

Robert composed a diplomatic letter home requesting that his overdrawn allowance be extended still further, so that he could travel south to Switzerland and Italy during the summer vacation. This granted, he set off on a rake's progress through Milan, Venice and the Adriatic. Despite love-sickness in Milan and sickness in Venice, he reckoned the adventure a success, and arrived back safely in Heidelberg in October.

The town and castle of Heidelberg

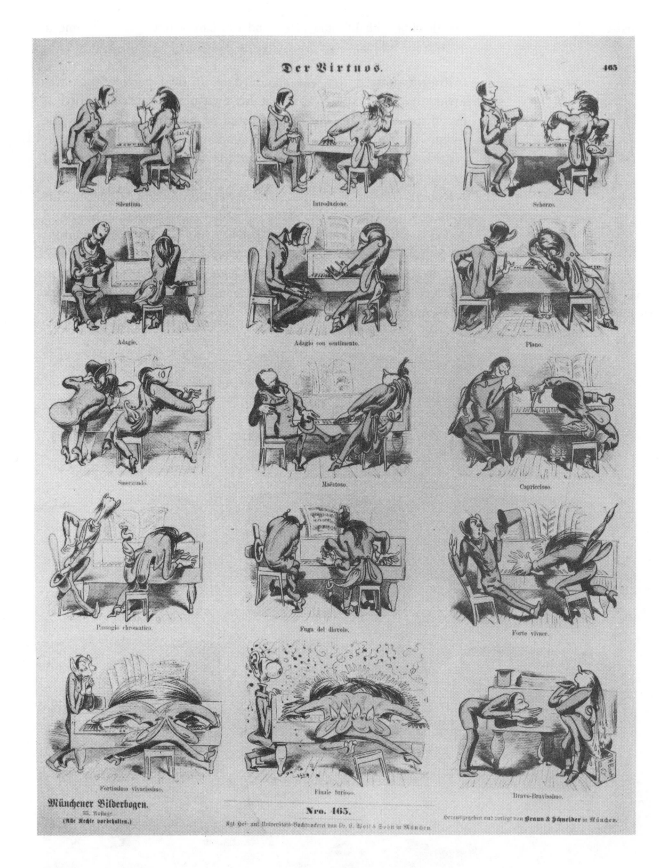

The Virtuoso, by W. Busch

Cartoon depicting Liszt's "eight hands"

A musical evening at the house of Professor Justus Thibaut

Robert now entered fully into Heidelberg's high life. Writing of sleigh parties, balls and friends, and claiming he was now 'the darling of Heidelberg', he overspent vastly. In February he wrote to his mother of large bills from his tailor and bootmaker:

then I must eat and drink; and I play the piano, and smoke, and sometimes, but not often, drive to Mannheim. I also require money for lectures, and want books and music, all of which costs an awful lot of money. Those wretched balls, tipping people, museum subscriptions, cigars – oh! those cigars – the piano-tuner, the laundress, the shoe-black, candles, soap, all my dear friends, who expect a wretched glass of beer, the man at the museum who brings the newspapers! I should completely despair if I weren't on the verge of desperation already!

Robert seemed to be applying himself spasmodically to law. But his overwhelming desire was to put down on paper the musical ideas teeming through his head. Robert had written to Wieck telling him just how strong the pull of music was. He talked of his systematic practice, his love of Schubert, and requested new music and the latest numbers of the music journal, the *Musikalische Zeitung*.

If he was due to give a soirée for friends, six or seven hours practice was often put in. Robert would even take a dummy keyboard with him when travelling into the countryside, to help perfect his technique. Schumann was invited to play before the Dowager Duchess of Baden, when he performed Moscheles' *Alexander Variations* with such skill that there was 'no end to the bravos and encores, and I really felt quite hot and uncomfortable'.

New compositions were appearing too. Finding that the name of a woman he met at a Mannheim ball, Meta Abegg, could be translated into musical notation, he sketched a variation on the notes A, Bflat, E, G, G. This is typical of his lifelong obsession for word-play and anagrams.

But as a law student, Schumann became increasingly lax. Fortunately Thibaut was a keen musician himself, and professor and student got on well together. Every week Thibaut organised a gathering of seventy or so people who joined to sing choruses from Handel, Bach or Palestrina, with the law professor accompanying at the piano. Robert was always a welcome guest.

Robert wrote:

Thibaut is a splendid, divine man. My most enjoyable hours are spent with him. When he has a Handel oratorio sung at his home . . . and accompanies enthusiastically on the piano, two big tears roll down from his fine big eyes beneath his beautiful silvery-white hair. And then he comes to me so delighted and serene, and presses my hand and is silent from sheer emotion. Often I don't know how a poor beggar like me has the honour to be allowed inside to listen in such a sacred house.

Paganini, from a sketch by Landseer

It is to Thibaut indeed that we owe the categorical statement that Robert had neither taste nor aptitude for law. For a time Schumann was at a loss as to how to communicate this news to his mother and his guardian. In the spring of 1830 he skirted round the issue, asking to stay on in Heidelberg for six months more. On Easter Sunday he travelled with two friends to Frankfurt to hear the virtuoso violinist Paganini play. As a result Robert was stimulated to start composing a set of variations.

But eventually the crucial issue had to be broached. He wrote to his mother, 30 July 1830:

32

Good morning, mama!

How can I describe my bliss at this moment? The spirit lamp is hissing under the coffee pot, the sky is indescribably clear and rosy, and the keen atmosphere of morning fills me with its presence. Besides, your letter lies before me and reveals a perfect treasury of good feeling, commonsense and virtue. My cigar tastes remarkably fine; in short the world is very lovely at times, if one could only get up early.

There is plenty of blue sky and sunshine in my life at present, but my guide, Rosen, is missing . . . I often feel very lonely, which sometimes makes me happy, sometimes miserable – it just depends. One can get on better without a lover than without a friend . . . My whole life has been twenty years' struggle between poetry and prose, or, if you like, music and law.

There is just as high a standard to be reached in practical life as in art. In the former, the ideal consists in the hope of plenty of work and a large, extensive practice; but what sort of prospect would there be in Saxony for such a man as myself, who has not noble birth, money or interest, and no affection for legal squabbles and pettiness? At Leipzig, I did not trouble my head about a career, but went dreaming and dawdling on, and never did any good.

Here I have worked harder, but both there and here I have been getting increasingly attached to art. Now I am standing at the crossroads, and scared about which way to go. My genius points towards art, which is, I'm inclined to think, the right path. But the fact is – now don't be angry with what I say – it always seemed to me as if you were putting obstacles in my way. You had very good reasons for doing so, and I understand them all perfectly, and we both agreed to call art an uncertain future and a doubtful way of earning your bread. There can certainly be no greater misery than to look forward to a hopeless, shallow, miserable existence which one has prepared for oneself . . . I am still at the height of youth and imagination, with plenty of ability to cultivate and ennoble art, and have come to the conclusion that with patience and perseverance and a good teacher I should in six years be as good as any pianist, for piano-playing is mere mechanism and execution.

. . . Now comes the question; 'To be, or not to be?' for you can only do one thing well in this life, and I am always saying to myself, 'Make up your mind to do one thing thoroughly well, and with patience and perseverance you are bound to achieve something.'

This battle against myself is now raging more fiercely than ever, my dear mother. Sometimes I am bold and confident in my own strength and power, but at other times I tremble to think of the long way I have come, and of the endless road which stretches before me. As for Thibaut, he long ago recommended me to take up art. I would be very grateful if you would write to him, and he would like it too, but unfortunately he left for Rome some time ago, so I will probably never speak to him again. . . .'

If I am to go in for music, I must leave at once and return to Leipzig, where Wieck, whom I thoroughly trust, and who can tell me what I am up to, would then carry on my education. Afterwards I ought to go to Vienna for a year, and, if possible, study under Moscheles. Now I have a favour to ask, dear mother, which I hope you will grant. *Write to Wieck yourself and*

33

Robert Schumann

ask him point-blank what he thinks of me and my career. Please let me have a SPEEDY answer, deciding the question, so that I can leave Heidelberg quickly, although I will be very sorry to leave it and my many friends and favourite haunts. *If you like you can enclose this letter to Wieck. In any case the question must be decided before Michaelmas*, and then I will pursue my purpose in life, whatever that may be, with fresh vigour and without weeping. You must agree that this is the most important letter I have ever written, so I trust you will not hesitate to comply with my request, for there is no time to lose.

Goodbye dearest mother, and don't worry. Heaven will help us if we help ourselves.

Ever your most loving son,

Robert Schumann

Johanna promptly wrote to Wieck:

Honoured Sir,

According to the request of my son, Robert Schumann, I take the liberty of applying to you about the future of this dear son. With trembling and deep anxiety I ask how you like Robert's plan, which the enclosed letter explains. It is not in accordance with my views; and I freely confess that I have great fears about Robert's future. Much effort is required to become a distinguished musician, or even to earn a living by music; because there are too many great artists before him; and, were his talents truly remarkable, it is, and always will be, uncertain whether he would attract applause or earn a secure future...

I cannot tell you how sad and depressed I feel when I think of Robert's future. He is a good man. Nature gave him intellectual gifts such as others have to struggle for, and he is not bad-looking. He has enough money to follow his studies without difficulties, and there is enough left to support him reasonably well until he can provide for himself. Now he wants to choose a profession which should have been started ten years ago... My three other sons are very angry, and insist that I refuse...

All rests on your decision – THE PEACE OF A LOVING MOTHER, THE WHOLE HAPPINESS OF LIFE of a young and inexperienced man who lives in a higher sphere and will have nothing to do with practical life. I know that you love music. Do not let your feelings argue for Robert, but think of his age, his fortune, his ability and his future...

Excuse the distraction of my letter; I am so overcome by all that has passed that I am soul-sick. Never was a letter so hard for me to write as this.

May you be happy! And send an answer soon to your

Humble servant.

C. Schumann

Wieck replied within days:

Honoured lady,

I hasten to answer your esteemed favour of the 7th inst., without further assuring you in advance of my warmest sympathy. But my answer can only

35

be quite short, since I am pressed by business of various kinds, and since I must talk over the greater part of it with your son, if a satisfactory result is to be attained. My suggestion would be that in the first place he should leave Heidelberg – that hotbed of the imagination – and return to our cold, flat Leipzig.

At present I merely say that I pledge myself within three years to turn your son Robert, by means of his talent and imagination, into one of the greatest pianists alive. He shall play with more warmth and genius than Moscheles, and on a grander scale than Hummel. The proof of this I offer to you in my eleven-year-old daughter whom I am now beginning to present to the world. As to composition, our Cantor Weinlig will no doubt be sufficient for present requirements.

But: 1. Robert very mistakenly thinks 'that the whole of piano-playing consists of pure technique'; what a one-sided view! . . . I confess that when – in the lessons which I gave him – I succeeded, after hard struggles and great contradictoriness on his part, after unheard-of pranks played by his unbridled fancy upon two people of pure rationality like ourselves, in convincing him of the importance of a pure, exact, smooth, clear, well-marked and elegant touch, my advice very often bore little fruit for the next lesson, and I had to begin again, with my usual affection for him, to expound the old theme, to show him once more the distinctive qualities of the music he had studied with me . . . Has our dear Robert changed – become more thoughtful, firmer, stronger and, may I say, calmer and more masculine? This does not appear from his letters.

2. I will not undertake Robert unless for a year he has an hour with me almost every day . . .

3. I believe that a piano virtuoso . . . can earn his living only if he gives lessons . . . Robert would be able to live very comfortably as a piano teacher, since he has a small income of his own . . .

4. Can Robert determine to study cold, dry theory, and everything to do with it, with Weinlig for two years? . . . Will Robert now decide, like my Clara, to devote some hours every day to writing exercises in three- and four-part composition? . . .

5. If Robert will not do all that I have said, then I ask: What part will he play, and what outlet will his imagination find? . . .

Most honoured friend, do not be anxious – compulsion is little use in such matters: we must do our bit as parents – God does the rest. If Robert has the courage and the strength to demolish my doubts when he is with me, then let him go in peace and give your blessing. In the meantime, you will be awaiting his answer to these few lines, the writer of which respectfully signs himself,

Your most devoted servant,

Fr Wieck

The die was cast. On 24 September 1830, Robert Schumann abandoned Heidelberg and the study of law. He made his way back to Leipzig and music.

3 Leipzig Again

Since the time when Johann Sebastian Bach held the post of Thomas Cantor, Leipzig had played a leading role in German musical life. A thriving commercial centre, famous for its bookshops, printing presses and libraries, the city had gradually built up its musical activities during the course of the eighteenth century. From the small concerts and recitals held in private rooms and coffee houses there grew a concert society which owed much of

J. A. Hiller

37

its success to its leader, JA Hiller. In 1781 the society bought the cloth hall – the Gewandhaus – in Leipzig's market square. The concerts which were held there confirmed Leipzig's claims to musical importance.

By the turn of the century there was also a smaller concert society, 'Euterpe', run by the bustling CG Müller. Many of its members also played with the Gewandhaus orchestra; but the Euterpe planned to restrict its repertoire, concentrating on the first performance of new works.

Leipzig was also rich in chamber music; there was a local opera company, and Breitkopf & Härtel, one of Germany's leading music publishers, had their headquarters in the city. In addition, the music journal founded by Gottfried Härtel, *Allgemeine musikalische Zeitung*, which helped form German musical tastes, was published in Leipzig.

The Gewandhaus, Leipzig

While still a law student, Robert had done little to explore Leipzig's musical life. When he returned, he was overwhelmed by it. At first he was overflowing with confidence; but soon the realisation that he had wasted the previous three years threw him into dejection.

Until Christmas 1830, Roberts letters home catalogued his woes. Restless, bored and uneasy he wrote: 'Of my old fire and energy barely the ashes remain'. As usual, he overspent, leaving no money for clothes, to get his haircut, his piano tuned or even to buy a revolver with which he threatened to shoot himself. He did, however, find enough money to have his portrait painted as a present for his mother.

But just before Christmas he wrote to his mother:

This contempt and waste of money is a wretched characteristic of mine. You would not believe how reckless I am — I often actually throw money away. I am always reproaching myself, and making good resolutions, but the next minute I've forgotten them, and am tipping someone eight groschen! Being away from home and travelling about have much to do with it; but most of the blame attaches to myself and my damned carelessness. And I fear it will never improve.

Robert was living at Wieck's house in Grimmaische Gasse, to benefit fully from the daily lessons and exercises laid down by Wieck. Wieck was undoubtedly a very difficult man — short-tempered, sharp-tongued, argumentative. He had been very poor as a child and as a student, and only managed to go to university through the charity of friends, and by living off regular helpings of 'charity soup'. This left him mean and embittered for life. He was largely self-taught as a musician, since he studied theology at university. As a piano teacher he worked out his own system, and his own set of technical exercises. He advocated a 'singing' touch, and a quiet keyboard style. He was selective in his approach, and would only take on a handful of promising students. He married in 1816, but the marriage, to Marianne Tomlitz, was not a success, and they were divorced when Clara, his second daughter, was only five.

Robert's teacher did not doubt his pupil's musical ability, or his romantic imagination. But he had little sympathy for his temperamental instability, his tendency to give in to the whim of the moment, and his inability to resist the habits of smoking and drinking. Wieck prided himself on making allowances for his pupils' foibles; but Schumann's moodiness, laziness and unruliness irritated him. Wieck also had his daughter's career to think of; when Robert was in one of his difficult moods, Wieck naturally paid less attention to him than to his gifted Clara.

Clara Wieck

Robert often felt that he was being snubbed by his teacher. When he heard at Christmas that Wieck and Clara were taking off on a month's concert tour, Robert suggested that he should go to the composer Hummel for lessons. He was surprised at Wieck's indignation, as he explained to his mother:

The other day I suggested to Wieck, in a light and airy kind of way, my plans about Hummel; but he took it badly, and asked me whether I mistrusted him, or what; and whether, in fact, he was not the best master? He saw I was startled by such needless anger, but we are now quite friendly again, and he treats me most affectionately, like his own child. You can hardly have a notion of his fire, his judgement, his view or art; and yet, when he speaks of his own or Clara's interests, he is as rude as a bear.

The following summer, when Wieck announced his intention of touring with Clara again, Robert wrote a tactless letter to Hummel, asking to become his pupil, and disparaging Wieck's methods. Robert's friends opposed such a move, since Hummel was considered extremely old-fashioned. But it was only by chance that the plans fell down. Nothing more was heard, either, of theory lessons with Weinlig.

Wieck insisted that Robert train to become an all-round musician, with a thorough grasp of harmony and counterpoint. This Robert steadfastly refused. Only in June 1831, after unsuccessful lessons with KG Kupsch, did he approach Heinrich Dorn, who began instructing him in thorough-base and counterpoint. According to Dorn, Schumann's first exercise was 'a model of part-writing in defiance of the rules'.

Robert was a difficult pupil. He realised that order and discipline were essential to musicianship; but the slightest whiff of academicism was enough to make him rebel petulantly. He complained to Wieck:

I shall never be able to get on with Dorn; he wants to persuade me that music is nothing but fugues. Good heavens, how different people are! But I certainly feel that theoretical studies have a good effect on me. Previously I noted down everything on the impulse of the moment; now I follow the course of ideas more. And sometimes stop short and look round to discover where I am.

Soon Dorn had heard enough about Robert's imagination, and by April 1832 Schumann was teacherless, except for Marpurg's primer on musical theory, and Bach's *Well-Tempered Clavier*. Only the latter he appreciated:

The advantage of this is great, and seems to have a strengthening moral

effect upon one's whole system, for Bach was a thorough man all over. There is nothing sickly or stunted about him, and his works seem to be written for eternity.

Meanwhile Robert was also at work on his novel *Die Davidsbünder* from which two characters, Florestan and Eusebius, with their contrasting sayings, frequently turn up in his diaries. In October 1831, for instance, he wrote in his diary:

Florestan has meanwhile become the friend of my heart, he shall really be my true self in the story.

In the same month Kistner published Robert's Opus 1, the 'ABEGG Variations'; but his most ambitious composition of 1831 was a piano sonata. In addition, inspired by incidents at the masked ball in Jean Paul's novel *Flegeljahre*, Robert completed a set of piano pieces entitled *Papillons*. Reviewing these and the ABEGG Variations, the poet Grillparzer wrote:

It is always pleasant to stand on one's own feet, and to need neither a crutch nor the shoulders of others. This is the first time we have encountered this, probably young, composer, who is one of the rarities of the age. He follows no school, but draws his inspiration entirely from himself, and does not adorn himself with strange feathers gathered in the sweat of his brow; on the contrary, he has created a new and ideal world for himself, in which he revels almost recklessly, and sometimes with quite original eccentricity.

The Wiecks returned home in May 1832, but Schumann did not go back to live with them, nor resume his piano lessons.

In his studies of technique, Schumann always had before him the example of Clara Wieck. Nine years his junior she already possessed an impressive mastery of the piano. Possibly Schumann was so impressed that he started speculating about a technical aid to short-cut exhausting keyboard exercises. Certainly a number of such technical devices appeared in the 1830s to improve pianists' technique.

We also know that at this time some mysterious tragedy occurred which cut short Schumann's career as a pianist. The traditional story is that, in a foolish attempt to 'equalize' his digits, Schumann invented some sort of sling, which restrained one finger while the others were being exercised. In the event the results were appalling; two tendons of his right hand were permanently damaged, preventing his continuing to play the piano in public.

But Schumann himself never specified the injury in detail. He speaks of 'Overdone technical studies. Laming of my right hand'. His letters only mention the damage in general terms. Much later, in 1889, Clara stated that the injury had been to her husband's right index finger, and was caused by practising at a dummy keyboard. The evidence is contradictory; what lies behind the mystery?

It is suggested that the so-called accident never actually happened. Rather, in an attempt to cure the syphilis which eventually brought about his death, Schumann damaged his nervous system by absorbing the poisonous mercury often prescribed in the nineteenth century. Other symptoms of syphilis later became evident, including numbness, speech impediments, ringing in the ears and giddiness.

A nineteenth-century
pianist

The full significance of the crippled hand took time to sink in. A number of cures were suggested, including animal baths – immersing his hand in cattle secretions – which Schumann found most unpleasant. He even expressed fears that the cattle's characteristics might pass into his personality. Seven years after the injury first occurred, Robert wrote to Clara:

Oh, Lord, why did you do just this to me? In me the whole of music is so complete and alive that I can play only painfully, with one finger straddling the others. It's terrible, and I have suffered again from it ever since.

But Robert did retain his sense of inner worth as a composer, 'my one object in life'. In fact 1832 was possibly one of his happiest periods. In July he wrote to his mother:

About 5am I jump out of bed like a deer and keep my account book, diary and correspondence in excellent state. Then I take turns to study, compose and read a bit ... Then comes dinner, and then I read either a French book or the paper. I habitually take a walk from three o'clock till six, usually by myself, towards Connewitz, where of course it's beautiful. I tell you – as I tell myself – 'You might live in paradise if you would accept life in all simplicity and soberness, and keep your demands within reasonable limits.' Then I frequently clap my hands in pleasure ... When I arrive home, at about six, I improvise till almost eight o'clock, then go to supper with Kömpel and Wolf, after which I return home.

Works finished during 1832 include his subsequently lost *Exercice fantastique* for piano, dedicated to Kuntzsch but vainly offered for publication; a set of six Intermezzi for piano, containing fragments of earlier works, and a set of twelve piano burlesques in the style of *Papillons*. By autumn Robert was ready for more ambitious work. He requested 'instruction in instrumentation' from Müller, the conductor of the Euterpe concerts, and asked him to go 'through ... a symphony movement of my own composition ... worked at almost entirely according to my own ideas and without guidance'. But no help was forthcoming, and a few days later Schumann took his symphonic score to Zwickau, where he stayed for most of the winter.

In November Clara and her father arrived in Zwickau to perform with the orchestra there, and Robert's symphonic movement received its first performance. But whereas Clara proved an instant success, Robert's symphonic effort did not. Particularly obvious were his shortcomings in orchestration. He wrote:

I often put in yellow instead of blue; but I consider this art so difficult that it will take long years' study to give me certainty and self control.

Ludwig van Beethoven

He proceeded to revise the piece, which was performed again at Schneeberg in February 1833.

Robert returned to Leipzig in March, taking up residence at Reidel's Garden. Though still only a young man of twenty-three, he was beginning to establish himself. His circle of acquaintances grew, and he spent his evenings with friends in restaurants or homes, talking about music and the arts. The group of friends were united in their idealism; they hated mediocrity and the dullness of much contemporary music. They campaigned for their idols, Beethoven and Schubert. Schumann himself wrote:

There is no music at all which is as psychologically remarkable in its progression and combination of ideas and its apparent leaps of logic as Schubert's. How few have been able, as he was, to impress a single individuality on such variety.

The young Turks also attacked the conservative press. In the summer of 1832: 'The thought awakened in a wild young heart: "Let us not look on idly, let us also lend our aid to progress. Let us again bring the poetry of art to honour among men".'

In plainer terms, they decided to start a new avant-garde music magazine, to fight philistines and champion romanticism. Robert approached Wieck to ask him to act as a director for the new journal, but the teacher was wary. After careful consideration, he eventually agreed.

The magazine, the *Neue Leipziger Zeitschrift für Musik* did not in fact appear until April 1834. Its first editor was Julius Knorr, but illness made him resign shortly and pass the job over to Robert Schumann. Robert's peculiar mark was soon evident in every issue. There was a characteristic rash of provocative articles, and inevitably many odd pseudonyms.

He also introduced the *Davidsbund*, a fictitious club made up of friends, dead and alive, united to attack the philistines. The opposing figures of Florestan and Eusebius, Schumann's alter egos, also appeared regularly, propagating his views. All this was partly natural playfulness, as Schumann explained to Dorn:

The *Davidsbund* is only intellectual and romantic, as you saw long ago. Mozart was as great a *bündler* as Berlioz. You too are a member though you never got your diploma.

But the two figures, Florestan and Eusebius, reveal clearly Schumann's own inner split. Robert was conscious of the conflicting claims of his inner self and of everyday life. The introspective Eusebius and the assertive Florestan spoke for these two contrasting worlds in the pages of the *Zeitschrift*. Occasionally

Frederic Chopin, by
Winterhalter

the two fused in a single, integrated personality, when he used the
pen-name 'Master Raro'.

A characteristic example of Schumann's use of the two personas
of Eusebius and Florestan comes in his famous review of Chopin,
published in 1832 in the *Allgemeine Musikalische Zeitung*, before the
Neue Zeitschrift first appeared:

47

Eusebius entered, not long ago. You know his pale face, and the ironical smile with which he awakens expectations. I sat with Florestan at the piano.

Florestan is, as you know, one of those rare musical minds that foresee cunning, novel or extraordinary things. But he encountered a surprise today. With the words, 'Hats off, gentlemen – a genius!' Eusebius laid down a piece of music. We were not permitted to see the title page. I turned over the leaves vacantly; the veiled enjoyment of music which one does not hear has something magical in it . . . 'Now play it', said Florestan. Eusebius consented; and in the recess of a window we listened. Eusebius played as though he were inspired, and . . . it seemed that the inspiration of the moment gave to his fingers a power beyond the ordinary measure of their cunning . . . But how surprised he was, when, turning to the title page he read, '. . . by Frederic Chopin', and with what astonishment we both cried, 'An Opus 2!' How our faces glowed as we wondered, exclaiming, '. . . Chopin, I never heard the name – who can he be? – at any rate a genius etc' . . . Heated with wine, Chopin and our own enthusiasm, we went on to Master Raro, who, with a smile, and displaying but little curiosity for Opus 2, said 'Bring me the Chopin! I know you and your new-fangled enthusiasm!'

Robert was by now very fond of Clara Wieck, who was still only fourteen. Her long concert tours and her father's assiduous training had left her very precocious. Robert wrote home in June 1833:

Clara is as fond of me as ever, and is just as she used to be, wild and enthusiastic, skipping and running about like a child, and saying the most profound things. It's wonderful to see how her gifts of mind and heart develop faster and faster . . . The other day, as we were walking back from Connewitz – we go for two or three hours' hike every day – I heard her say to herself: 'Oh how happy I am! How happy!' Who would not rejoice to hear that?

On the road there are many bits of stone lying in the middle of the path. When I'm talking, I tend to look up rather than down, so she always comes behind, gently tugging my coat at each rock, to stop me falling. But this doesn't prevent her keep stumbling herself.

In September Robert moved and took up rooms at 21 Burgstrasse. He heard in quick succession that his sister-in-law Rosalie and his brother Julius had died. These deaths upset him seriously. He experienced 'violent rushes of blood to the head, inexpressible nervousness, shortness of breath, sudden faintness'. He seems to have thought of throwing himself from his fourth floor window. The result of this was that he moved to the first floor, and acquired a lifelong dread of living high up. He had to persuade a friend to sleep in the same room to stop him doing anything desperate.

Robert's diary shows he thought he was going mad, and he wrote to his mother:

I won't say anything about the last few weeks. I was more a statue than anything, with neither heat nor cold.

But by applying himself to hard work he apparently pulled himself slowly out of the blackness. From March 1834 he was heavily occupied with the *Zeitschrift* as well as with composing. Robert had already written articles for several journals, and as editor of the *Zeitschrift* became an influential and perceptive critic.

Bach monument in Leipzig

Schumann's manuscript of *The Two Grenadiers*

4 Clara

Although now very busy as both journalist and composer, Robert yearned for affection. He soon fell for seventeen-year-old Ernestine von Fricken, who came to Leipzig in April 1834 to live in at the Wiecks', and to study with Clara's father. She had grown up in the little town of Asch with her father, Baron von Fricken, and was the illegitimate daughter of Countess Zedtwitz.

Schumann was infatuated:

(She was) a wonderfully pure, child-like character, delicate and thoughtful. She is truly devoted to me, and loves anything artistic. She's extraordinarily musical. Everything, in short, that I would want in my wife.

At the beginning of September 1835 Robert and Ernestine were secretly engaged. Within days, Baron von Fricken heard that something was afoot, arrived in Leipzig, and took Ernestine back to Asch. After secret discussions, the engagement was broken off by mutual agreement. Possibly Robert had been kept in the dark about Ernestine's origins.

In any event, the affair had a catalytic effect on Robert's music. He had the idea of writing a series of piano pieces based on the letters ASCH; these he later turned into *Carnaval*. He also composed some piano variations on a theme provided by Baron von Fricken.

But Robert's friend Schunke had fallen seriously ill. Unable to bear the sight, Robert went back to Zwickau again, only returning to Leipzig in December to negotiate a change of publisher for the *Zeitschrift*. From the beginning of 1835 the journal was published by the Leipzig firm of JA Barth.

Late in 1835 Mendelssohn arrived in Leipzig to take over as music director of the Gewandhaus. Still only twenty-six, Mendelssohn was the wonder of the age, and Schumann felt an immediate attraction when they met at Wieck's house. Following the young newcomer's debut in Leipzig, Schumann wrote praising him in the 'Letters of an Enthusiast' column of his *Zeitschrift*. Schumann did however venture to criticise Mendelssohn's use of the baton; he believed that an orchestra should function as a 'republic' and that rigidity should be avoided.

Mendelssohn always harboured reservations about Schumann. He had a strong prejudice against critics and journalists – people who wrote about music rather than creating it. A complete professional himself, he also objected to Schumann's apparently dilettante approach to music.

At about this time, too, Robert met both Chopin and Ignaz Moscheles at the Wiecks'. Throughout the autumn of 1835 Schumann was a regular visitor at Wieck's home, seeing much of Clara, who was now sixteen. He had been following her career as a virtuoso closely since she was nine; when he was depressed, she cheered him up. Their latent affection was now becoming increasingly evident. Robert had now finished his first piano sonata, dedicated 'to Clara, by Florestan and Eusebius'. The

Chopin, a sketch by George Sand

evening before Clara set out on an important concert tour, Robert came to wish her well, and kissed her goodbye. They saw each other again in Zwickau, and kissed again. In the new year Robert travelled to Dresden, where he knew Clara was spending a holiday without her father, and made a declaration of his love.

On 4 February 1836 Schumann's mother died. Even in this tragedy, he could write to Clara:

Your radiant image shines through the darkness and helps me bear everything better . . . Perhaps your father won't refuse if I ask his blessing. Of course there is a lot needing thought and arranging. But I put great trust in our guardian angel. Fate always intended us for one another . . .

Schumann seems to have thought Clara's father would welcome him as his son-in-law. He was wrong. Hearing that Robert and Clara had been meeting behind his back, Wieck was enraged, and wrote to Robert insisting that all relations be severed. At the same time he distracted Clara's attention by flaunting her new singing teacher, Karl Banck.

Clara, only just sixteen, was regarded by her father as a mere child. Wieck had nurtured her talents, and now saw her on the threshold of an outstanding career. He was not going to stand by and watch her marry Schumann, who he knew, to his own irritation, had neglected his training and squandered his resources.

Naturally Robert was desperate. Extravagant spending sprees led to pleas to his brothers for money. He started drinking heavily again, and his generally uncouth habits led to a noisy argument with his landlady. Finally he wrote to her:

Why should I moan at you about ruined plans, deserved and undeserved sorrows, and youthful griefs which meet all of us? I have some wonderful hours at the piano, talking to charming people, and intend to achieve even greater things. But it is this very way of thinking that finishes in presumptuousness . . . Then the rot sets in. I know perfectly well what is needed to bring together these contracting moods – a loving woman.

To understand Wieck's attitude, we need to examine his feelings about Clara. She represented his special creation, his life's work. He had laboured with her for long years at the keyboard. She had finally emerged as his best pupil, the star exemplar of his techniques. At the same time she now represented a valuable commercial asset. She simultaneously fed Wieck's wallet and his ego.

But Robert, for his part, was emotionally barred from recognising Wieck's motivation. He wrongly surmised that Wieck was personally opposed to Robert Schumann, whereas the older man would have turned on anyone who stood between him and his daughter. Whoever the enemy, Wieck would have used every weapon to hand – abuse, lies, libel and even violence – to maintain his hold over his daughter.

When Clara and her father returned to Leipzig in April, Robert was forbidden to see her. When Robert sent her the first engraving of a new piano sonata she responded by sending back all his love letters, and requesting hers back too.

In a further piano sonata, started in June, Robert expressed something of his despair at being parted from Clara. It was considerably revised before it was finally published as his *Fantasie* in 1839, with a quotation from Schlegel at its head:

Through all earth's motley dream, one soft note can be heard by him who listens stealthily.

Robert later wrote to Clara:

I think the first movement is more impassioned than anything I have ever written – a deep lament for you.

Schumann's *Fantasie* was dedicated to Liszt, who reminisced about it to one of his own pupils:

I remember the first time I played it to the great composer. He remained perfectly silent in his chair . . . which rather disappointed me. So I asked him what impression my performance of the work had made . . . He asked me to proceed with the March, after which he would give me his criticism. I played the second movement so effectively that Schumann jumped out of his chair, and with tears in his eyes cried, 'Göttlich, our ideas are completely identical as to the rendering of these movements. But you, with your magic fingers, have carried my ideas into practice.'

In May 1837, after another long tour, Clara arrived back in Leipzig. Not long afterwards Banck, like Schumann before him, was rejected by Wieck as a suitor for Clara. At this time Schumann's disappointment seems to have turned to malice. He declared himself ready to avenge himself on Clara. But this was only a temporary mood; in a letter to her in August, with words 'cold and serious, yet so beautiful', Robert protested she remained 'the dearest in the world'.

His feelings were echoed by his beloved. On 14 August they became secretly engaged. Clara wrote to him:

So one little 'Yes' is all you ask? What an important little word it is! Surely a heart so filled with inexpressible love as mine can speak it freely? I can indeed speak it. My innermost soul breathes it unceasingly to you.

Emboldened by this, on 13 September, Clara's eighteenth

Robert Schumann

birthday, Robert wrote to Wieck asking for his consent to their marriage. He argued that his prospects were greatly improved, and his stability enhanced; 'You owe it to my position, my talent and my character'.

Wieck's response was unchanged. What he wanted was a wealthy husband who could protect Clara from financial cares. Robert was once more in the depths of despondency:

My interview with your father was terrible. He was frigid, hostile, confused and contradictory at once. Truly his method of stabbing is original, for he drives in the hilt as well as the blade . . . Do all you can to find a way out. I will follow like a child. How my poor head swims. I could laugh from anguish. This cannot continue very much longer – my health won't bear it. God keep me from despair!

But later Robert took a more calm attitude:

If he drives us to extremes by continuing to refuse his agreement for a year and a half or two years more, we will have to take the law into our own hands. In that event, a magistrate could marry us. God grant it shall not come to that . . . Please let me hear a few soothing, kind words from you soon. My picture of you is clearer and lovelier now than when I was writing this morning; and your 'steadfast', repeated three times, is a message from Heaven.

But Clara and her father were away on tour for much of the winter of 1837/38. She achieved the peaks of acclaim in Vienna. Robert wrote longingly again in March:

If only you knew how much I value your views, not only about art, but about everything going on. How much your letters cheer me! Tell me about everything going on around you: the people, the towns, the customs. You are so observant and I adore following your reflections. It isn't good to get too self-absorbed, as you can when you lose sight of the outside world. There is so much beauty, richness and novelty in our world. If I had told myself that more frequently in the past, I would have achieved more, and got further.

For Robert, life in Leipzig continued to be largely occupied with duties connected with the *Zeitschrift*. He continued to take his editorial and critical roles seriously, and devoted much care to the journal.

Following his reconciliaition with Clara in 1837, Robert's first new work was the *Davidsbündlertänze*, which he published at his own cost. He headed the music:

Along the way we go are mingled weal and woe; in weal, though glad, be grave, though sad, be brave.

Clara Schumann

Robert Schumann

Signatures of Robert and
Clara Schumann, with
music written by them

Each piece had an F or an E (Florestan or Eusebius) at the
beginning; in four instance both letters appeared. For the ninth
piece Schumann wrote: 'Here Florestan keeps silent, but his lips
were quivering with emotion'. The last had the inscription 'Quite
superfluously Eusebius remarked the following, but all the time
great joy spoke from his eyes.'

To Clara he wrote:

There are many wedding thoughts in the dances, which were suggested by
the most delicious excitement I can remember. I will explain them to you
one day.

Later he continued:

Have you not received the *Davidsbündlertänze* . . . I sent them to you last
Saturday week . . . They are my own property, but my Clara will
understand everything in the dance. For they are dedicated to her, and
more emphatically than any of my other pieces . . . If ever I was happy at
the piano it was while composing them.

Despite this fond belief, Clara did not always follow the complex
allusions in the dances.

In 1838, Robert followed these piano pieces with *Novelleten*.
These finished, he wrote to Clara:

I've found out nothing sharpens the imagination as much as expecting and

59

Vienna in 1848

longing for something, and this is how I've been for the last few days. I have been waiting for your letter, and as a result have written books-ful of pieces – amazing, crazy, sober stuff. You'll stretch your eyes when you open it up. In fact, I sometimes feel as if I'm simply bursting with music. But before I forget, let me tell you what else I've written. Whether it was an echo of something you once said to me, 'that sometimes I seemed to you like a child', at any rate, I suddenly got inspired, and knocked off about thirty funny little pieces, from which I have chosen twelve. They'll amuse you, but of course you must forget you're a performer . . . They all explain themselves, and as well as that, they're as easy as you can imagine.

Schumann also wrote to Clara about his series of piano pieces entitled *Kreisleriana*:

Play my *Kreisleriana* very often. A positively wild love is in some of the movements, and your life, and mine, and the way you look.

Schumann's mind was overflowing with music so that he could barely get it all down on paper:

I'm affected by everything that goes on in this world, and think it all over in my own way, politics, literature, and people. Then I yearn to express my feelings, and find an outlet for them in music. That is why my music is sometimes difficult to understand, because it is linked to remote interests;

60

and sometimes striking, because everything extraordinary that happens impresses me, and forces me to express it in music. That is why so few modern pieces satisfy me, because apart from all their faults in construction, they deal with the very lowest music feelings, and with vulgar lyrical outpourings. The best of what they do here doesn't match my earliest music. Theirs might be a flower, but mine is a poem, infinitely more spiritual. Theirs is a mere natural impulse, mine results from political consciousness.

But at Easter Robert wrote to Clara:

It's very odd, but if I write much to you, as I'm doing now, I can't compose. The music all goes to you.

When the Wiecks returned to Leipzig, Robert tried to spend as much time as he could with Clara. They even toyed with the idea of moving to Vienna, and getting the *Zeitschrift* published there. Wieck's main ostensible objection to Robert's marrying Clara was now financial. If the couple were to settle in Vienna, Clara could expect to double her income from concert fees, and Robert's royalties would also rise appreciably. But such plans were soon dismissed as impractical.

5 Marriage

Keen to explore the possibilities of moving to Vienna, Robert visited the city in September 1838. But he soon found it irritated him; he hated the gossip and back-biting he encountered, and looked in vain for 'artists who not only play one or two instruments pretty well, but are big enough to understand Shakespeare and Jean Paul'. He tried to obtain a permit to publish his *Zeitschrift* in Vienna, and even hoped to bring out the first Viennese issue by January 1839. But this was over-optimistic. He had enough problems finding a publisher, and the outspoken tone of his magazine made for insurmountable problems with the censor. Exasperated, Robert resolved to return to Leipzig early in 1839. However his time in Austria was not entirely wasted; Robert did find a little time to compose some piano pieces. He then went on to work on a 'big romantic sonata', later titled *Faschingsschwank aus Wien*.

From Vienna Robert sent a number of little verses to Clara, romantic expressions of his devotion:

> A maid of twenty and not yet a wife,
> A man of thirty who is but a lover,
> Are losing fast, and never may recover,
>   The spring of life.
>
> There is a bride, a faithful bride, for me,
> And in her eyes, for any man to see,
> Is a sure gage of women's loyalty.

Robert's trip did have one important 'serendipity'. Calling on Schubert's brother Ferdinand, a poor schoolteacher with eight children, Robert discovered a mass of unpublished Schubert manuscripts, including operas, four masses and five symphonies, all of which he took to the music publishers Breitkopf and Härtel. The hoard included Schubert's 'Great' C major symphony, and Schumann sent the score of this to Mendelssohn in Leipzig, where in due course he conducted the first performance, at the Gewandhaus, on 21 March 1839. It was a triumph. Schumann described it as 'the greatest achievement in instrumental music since Beethoven'.

Franz Schubert

Just as Robert was setting out from Vienna to return to Leipzig, he heard that his brother Eduard was seriously ill. Robert claimed later that he had premonitions of tragedy and wrote to Clara:

I told you about a premonition I had. It haunted me while I was absorbed in my new composition . . . While I was composing I kept seeing funerals, coffins, and unhappy, despairing faces. When I had finished and was trying to think of a title, the only one that came to me was 'Corpse Fantasy'. Isn't that odd? I was so moved by the composition that tears came to my eyes, and yet I didn't know why . . .

His brother died in April, and his death was a heavy blow to Robert. Eduard had been very close to him. When Robert arrived in Leipzig, Clara was away playing in Paris. In the family crisis that ensued, Robert even briefly considered abandoning for a while his career as a composer to take care of the Schumann publishing and bookselling business.

To add to his worries, Clara now began echoing her father's demands for financial security as a preliminary to getting married. Robert was badly hurt by this turn-about. Clara's ability as a pianist was now recognised throughout Europe; by contrast, Robert was still relatively obscure, although from the outset he had always assured her that his music would become famous.

Robert himself believed he already had enough money for the couple to live on, though possibly not with the elegance Wieck demanded. Robert's own doubts about marriage centred rather on his own personal worth. On 3 June 1839 he wrote to Clara:

In the years to come, you'll often worry about me, so much is still needed to make a man of me. I'm often too restless, too childish, too yielding, and I often abandon myself to whatever gives me pleasure, without considering other people. In short, I have my bad days when there is nothing to be done with me.

But Wieck still resisted all pleas for his consent. Eventually, in September 1839 Clara signed an affidavit applying for her father's consent to be set aside. She said later:

The moment I signed was the most important of my whole life. I set my name down with resolution, and was inexpressibly happy.

Wieck was outraged. He refused to have Clara in his house, and she had to go to live with her mother in Berlin. Beside himself, Wieck wrote to dealers telling them not to let Clara play their pianos, in case she should damage the action. He attempted to scare off her audiences by spreading reports of 'shameless' behaviour. Whenever he met Robert in the street, he spat in his face. Finally he drew up a document listing five quite impossible requirements before he would agree to the marriage:

1. The couple could not live in Saxony.
2. The 7000 thalers already earned by Clara would be forfeit; only 4½% would be given to her.
3. Schumann's statement of his income must be guaranteed by the courts.
4. Schumann must not have any communication with Wieck until the latter agreed.
5. Clara would lose all inheritance rights from her father.

These terms were completely unrealistic, and Robert and Clara sent a Leipzig lawyer named Einert to try to effect a conciliation. But Wieck shrieked that he would have his way 'though it meant the destruction of thirty people'. In December there was a second conciliation attempt; the parties met in court, and Wieck became so wild that the judge had to silence him. With no-one to represent him, Wieck's case was rejected by the judge, although he was given permission to appeal. After further alarms and excursions in August, the court finally found in favour of the young couple. On 16 August 1839 the banns were published.

Leipzig

Just before the wedding took place Robert and Clara exchanged a pair of moving letters. On 29 August Robert wrote to Clara:

I have two things at heart that I must say to you before the eternal Yes, my Clara. You said not long ago, as a joke, 'You know . . . my tendency to be jealous' . . . I know very well that your reproach was aimed at me . . . But now I don't want you to be afraid of the future and to take me for an Othello at heart . . . If there are others of whom I might be jealous in the future, name them to me, so that you shan't be too proud in your belief in my jealousy.

The other thing . . . we have several times had downright quarrels, and that was a good thing. But when next day, or a few hours later, I've wanted to explain everything quietly to you, you have flared up again, and so violently that I have often been frightened. My little Clara, you must get out of this habit. You can't keep going over old squabbles . . .

And while I'm talking about it . . . here is a third plea before the wedding: I've told you what I'm afraid of in you; now tell me what you find wrong in me. I want to reform myself . . .

Clara replied a few days later:

I cannot think of anything I find wrong in you, but if I do I will tell you frankly, as I have already done several times. And then I'd rather not do it in writing since I don't always put it right . . . If it absolutely must be before the wedding, let's have a really good squabble . . . Otherwise, enough of that!

The wedding finally took place on 12 September, the day before Clara's twenty-first birthday. After that she would in any case be free of her father's will. Possibly Robert chose the day as a final signal of defiance to his new father-in-law.

Clara, at least, was enraptured:

What can I write about this day? We were married at Schönefeld at ten o'clock. First came a chorale, and then a short address by the preacher, Wildenhahn, a friend from Robert's younger days. His sermon was simple but heartfelt. My whole soul was filled with gratefulness to the One who had brought us safely over many rocks and precipices to meet at last. I prayed fervently that He would preserve my Robert to me for many, many years. Indeed, the thought that I might one day lose him is enough to send me out of my mind. Heaven avert this calamity! I couldn't bear it. . . .

There was a little dancing, no superfluous gaiety, but everyone's face shone with genuine satisfaction. The weather was wonderful. Even the sun, who had hidden his face for many days, shed his warm beams on us as we drove to church, as if to bless our union. It was a day without blemish, and I may enter it in this book as the fairest and most momentous of my life.

During the previous litigation, Robert's main consolation was the arrival in Leipzig of Franz Liszt. He wrote to Clara:

I am tired out with all the excitement of the last few days . . . As long as Liszt is here, I cannot do much work . . . He said yesterday: 'I feel as if I have known you twenty years', and I have just the same feeling towards him. We have got to the stage of being as rude as we like to each other, and I have frequent cause to take advantage of the privilege since he is simply too capricious and has been spoilt by his period in Vienna . . . I have at last had a chance of hearing Liszt's wonderful playing, which alternates between a fine frenzy and utter delicacy. But this world is not mine, my little Clara. Art, as we know it – you when you play, I when I compose – has an intimacy and charm that is worth more to me than all Liszt's splendid tinsel.

Schumann meanwhile resumed earlier enquiries about a doctor's degree, approaching a friend called Keferstein who had influence at the University of Jena. Keferstein replied that the university would grant him a doctorate, and Schumann began to think about submitting a thesis on Shakespeare. But he was overjoyed when on

An afternoon with Liszt, by Kriehuber.
Left-right: Kriehuber, Berlioz, Czerny, Liszt, Ernst

28 February he received an honorary degree for his work as a composer, critic and editor.

The impending court action also seems to have stimulated Robert's creative impulses. In May 1840 Robert wrote to Clara that he had been composing 'so much that it really seems quite uncanny at times. I can't help it, and should like to sing myself to death like a nightingale'.

After an interval of some twelve years, Schumann now returned to writing *lieder*. The first sign of this new flood of songs was a setting of the 'Fool's Song' from Twelfth Night, in February. By the end of the same month, Robert had set Heine's nine *Liederkreis*, which were followed by a number of Heine songs, including the great *Dichterliebe*.

The Schumanns set up house at 5 Inselstrasse. As time passed, Wieck gradually realised he had greatly underestimated Robert.

Heinrich Heine

Clara Schumann

Clara bore him a succession of grandchildren, and his natural wish to see them contributed to the effecting of a reconciliation in 1843. Wieck wrote to his son-in-law:

Dear Schumann,

Tempora mutantur et nos mutamur in eis.

In the face of Clara and the world we can no longer keep apart from each other. You are, in any case, the father of a family – do we need a longer explanation? We were always united where art was concerned – I was even your teacher – my verdict decided your present course in life. There is no need for me to assure you of my sympathy for your talent and with your fine and genuine aspirations. In Dresden there joyfully awaits you,

Your father

Fr Wieck

As a result of this conciliatory letter, the two families joined for Christmas at the Wiecks' home in Dresden.

6 Robert and Clara

The next few years seem to have been among the happiest in Schumann's life. Free of anxiety and sure of Clara's love, he turned to work with a new confidence. He proved a devoted husband and his close affection was returned by Clara. The Schumanns loved reading together – Goethe, Jean Paul or Shakespeare. They also kept a joint diary; an entry by Robert for August 1841 is typical:

Clara is studying Beethoven (not to mention Schumann) with enthusiasm. She has helped me greatly to arrange my symphony. In between she is reading Goethe's life, but still chops beans when needed. Music she cares for more than anything, and that gives me enormous joy.

Robert and Clara are often popularly pictured as an ideal couple, each serving as a complement for the other. Yet it was not a relationship without stress. There was frequently a clash of artistic interest, causing damaged feelings on both sides. Clara's piano playing was the first to suffer. She wrote in her diary:

My playing is getting all behind, as always happens when Robert's composing. I can't find a single hour in the day to myself. If only I didn't get so behind.

Robert was all too aware of the problem, and built up a reservoir of guilt. Robert also found separation from his wife extremely threatening, although to tour with her made him more acutely aware of her greater popularity. Money had to be earned, although he found it almost impossible to write any music while Clara was away from home.

But Schumann was able to be philosophical about their marriage:

Well, so must it be when artists marry. We cannot have everything; and after all the chief thing is the happiness which remains over and above, and we are happy indeed in that we possess one another and understand and love with all our hearts.

In December 1839 Robert had written to Clara:

Robert and Clara
Schumann

I have been in paradise today! They played at the rehearsal a symphony of Franz Schubert's. How I wish you had been there, for I cannot describe it

70

A nineteenth-century orchestra

to you. The instruments all sing like remarkably intelligent human voices, and the scoring is worthy of Beethoven. Then the length, the heavenly length, of it! It is a whole four-volume novel, longer than the choral symphony. I was supremely happy, and had nothing left to wish for, except that you were my wife, and that I could write such symphonies myself.

Schumann's enthusiasm was reflected in the article on Schubert's symphony for the *Neue Zeitschrift*:

. . . Save in a few of Beethoven's works I have nowhere in the treatment of instruments observed so striking and deceptive a resemblance to the voice; . . . Another proof of the genuine, mature inspiration of this symphony is its complete independence of the Beethoven symphonies. Here you can see how correct, how prudent in judgment Schubert's genius reveals itself. As if conscious of his own more modest powers, he avoids imitating the grotesque forms, the bold proportions which we find in Beethoven's later works; he gives us a creation of the most graceful form possible, yet full of novel intricacies; he never strays far from the central point and always returns to it . . . It would not give us others any pleasure to analyse the separate movements, for to give an idea of the fictional character that pervades the whole symphony the entire work should be copied.

13 October 1841 there is a brief entry in Robert's diary: 'Afternoon symphonic attempts'. This was the news that Clara had been waiting for impatiently. A year before she had written:

It would be best if he composed for orchestra. His imagination cannot find enough scope with the piano, and his music is all orchestral in feeling. My greatest wish is for him to compose for orchestra – that's his field. May I succeed in leading him to it.

Friedrich Rückert

In the event, this was a false start, and Robert continued with his spate of lieder. The songs of this year were collected in *Lieder und Gesänge*, and three books of *Romanzen und Balladen*. The last works of this 'year of song' were the settings of Rückert's '*Gedicht aus Liebesfrühling*'.

It was still the romantic poets who inspired Schumann. Until now he normally composed at the keyboard; now music began to come ready-formed into his head. He wrote of this fruitful period: 'My work has become gayer, gentler and more melodious'. Yet, since his first symphonic attempts, he had been striving for a larger form. Stimulated by hearing Schubert's 'Great' Symphony, Robert finally started work in January 1841 on a symphony in B flat. The work went well. Robert wrote:

The symphony has given me so many hours of sheer bliss. I'm full of gratitude to my guardian angel for letting me finish a big work with such ease, and in such a short time.

He later told the composer, Spohr:

It was inspired, if I may say so, by the spirit of spring which seems to possess us all anew every year, regardless of our age. The music is not intended to describe or picture anything specific, but I am convinced that spring shaped the form it has taken.

On 31 March 1841 Mendelssohn conducted the first performance of Schumann's *Spring Symphony* at the Gewandhaus. At the same concert Clara played Chopin's second piano concerto, as well as some of Robert's piano solos. There had previously been problems in rehearsal – Robert had forgotten that hand-horns and 'natural' trumpets could not manage the notes he asked of them. The actual premiere was a success – though not so overwhelming as the Schumanns like to think. Robert was intoxicated:

How much I enjoyed hearing the symphony performed. And so did others; for it was received with more sympathy than I think any modern symphony since Beethoven.

There was a cooler review in the *Leipziger Zeitung*, and Schumann wrote bitterly to the critic EF Wenzel:

Was that your essay? I was greatly hurt by it. I had been so happy. To point to the future, after a work performed with such enthusiasm, and with such cold words. And yet it surprised you? I hate such expressions like poison.

Despite such coolness, Robert was confident enough to push ahead with other works for the orchestra. On 6 December there

Louis Spohr

came the first performance of his Overture, Scherzo and Finale. Then followed a Fantasie in A Minor for piano and orchestra, which later formed the first movement of his A minor piano concerto.

On 1 September 1841 Clara gave birth to a daughter, Marie. Robert was overjoyed; but her birth served to increase Clara's dilemma. She now had to deal with the competing roles of mother and virtuoso:

I owe it to my reputation not to retire completely. It's a feeling of duty towards you and towards myself which speaks in me. I shall be quite forgotten, and in a few years' time, when possibly we shall want to tour, who can tell what other things in art people will be interested in.

As a birthday present, Robert gave Clara the manuscript of a second symphony, this time in D minor. He had started work on it in September, and the first performance came in December. It was not well received, and Schumann was naturally disappointed. In due course he revised it heavily, and eventually published it in 1851, when it was numbered as his fourth symphony.

Robert meanwhile began work on yet another symphony:

It was almost too much at once, I think. But that doesn't matter. I know the music is in no way inferior to my first . . .

Yet Schumann has never been regarded as a successful symphonist. One critic has written:

To call Schumann one of the Cinderellas among the important nineteenth-century symphonists may seem severe. Yet what are the facts? Though much more firmly established than Bruckner's and Mahler's, his symphonies – to say nothing of the rest of his orchestral music – enjoy far less popularity than those of Schubert, Mendelssohn, Brahms and Tchaikovsky. To the public at large he is the composer of delightful piano miniatures, of the Piano Concerto and the Piano Quintet. In the sphere of the *Lied* we greet him as one of Schubert's few great successors – an eloquent and inspired singer of the bliss and sorrow of romantic love. Yet Schumann the symphonist and orchestral writer takes a back seat in our esteem. In the programmes of orchestral concerts his symphonies and overtures make but rare appearances, for the simple truth is that their lack of brilliance and generally ineffective orchestration make it difficult for conductors to earn kudos with them . . . Weingartner considered the symphonies far more effective if played as piano duets. . . . We do not value them for their classical attributes but for the romantic spirit that keeps breaking in . . . By nature a miniaturist, his self-chosen domain was first the short self-contained piano piece and song.

Anton Bruckner (1824-1896)

Gustav Mahler (1860-1911)

J. S. Bach playing the organ

In 1841 an aspiring young composer from Munich named Johann Herzog sent some of his work to Robert Schumann for his criticism. In his friendly and helpful reply, Robert reveals something of his personal approach to composition:

You seem to be particularly at home on the organ. This is a great advantage, and the greatest composer in the world has written most of his most glorious compositions for this instrument. But, on the other hand, the organ rather tempts one to a certain comfortable way of composing, because almost anything sounds well on it directly. At any event, do not write too many small things, and try your hand at something bigger, such as a fugue, a toccata etc., of which Bach has left us the highest examples.

But if you don't want to become exclusively a composer of organ music, try a piano sonata or a string quartet, and above all write for the voice. That gets you on more than anything, and brings out the innermost qualities of the musician. . . . If your courage fails you, strengthen it by turning to our great German masters – for instance Bach, Handel and Beethoven.

In 1842 the Schumanns were invited to Bremen and Hamburg. On this occasion Robert travelled with Clara, to avoid habitual anxiety on being parted from her. A performance of his symphony was received politely, but Clara's playing was rapturously acclaimed. Clara was keen to continue her tour to Copenhagen, but Robert, acutely aware of his role as Clara's appendage, was equally keen to draw the tour to an end. Everywhere they travelled, from now on he pointedly refused to conduct his symphony, using the excuse of his short-sightedness.

Clara eventually went on to Denmark by herself, throwing Robert into such despair that composition was out of the question. He spent his time back in Leipzig working on the *Zeitschrift*, drowning his sorrows in 'beer and champagne', working at counterpoint and fugue, and brooding over whether to take Clara to the United States. Robert's gloom deepened when he heard that Wieck was spreading rumours that the young couple had already parted.

Happily, Clara's return marked a further creative outburst – this time of chamber music. In his solitude, Robert had been carefully studying the string quartets of Haydn, Mozart and Beethoven. Now, with Clara safe home again, he started work on some 'quartet essays'. He started an A minor quartet in early June, and by July had completed three quartets. This frenzy of writing was not allowed to get in the way of a savage piece of journalism in the *Zeitschrift* attacking his one-time rival as suitor, Banck. A similar libellous attack on Gustav Schilling was punished by the authorities with a fine of five thalers.

In August Robert and Clara went to Carlsbad and Marienbad for
a break. Robert returned to Leipzig to complete a piano quintet
and, despite 'constant fearful sleepless nights', a piano quartet.

Finally the frenzy of the previous two years caught up with
Schumann, and he was overcome by 'weakness of the nerves'.
Composition ceased, and Robert was seriously worried about the
lack of money and the needs of his family. He wrote in May 1843:

Times have changed with me . . . I used to be indifferent to the amount of
attention I received, but a wife and children have put a different
complexion on everything. It becomes vital to think of the future, desirable
to see the fruits of my labour – not the artistic fruits, but the mundane
fruits of life.

In April 1843 Schumann was appointed Professor of piano, composition and score-reading at Leipzig's Music School, which gave him a way of improving his financial situation. But Robert was not a success as a teacher. He was too introspective and quiet, and failed to interest his students.

Hector Berlioz, a caricature by Carjat

Mikhail Ivanovitch
Glinka

Early in 1843 Berlioz came to Leipzig. A tall wild-looking Frenchman with startling red hair and piercing eyes, Schumann had always supported him. In return, Berlioz, who was usually antagonistic towards German composers, greeted the first performance of Robert's piano quintet with generous approval.

It was at this time that Wieck's overtures of reconciliation came. Perhaps Robert's increased renown and the arrival of grandchildren helped prompt them.

In February 1843 Robert began work on a setting of Thomas Moore's 'Paradise and the Peri', 'an oratorio . . . for bright, happy people'. He saw the work as the most important he had yet undertaken. But, once he had finished it, he wrote little else this year. In December he directed the first orchestral rehearsals of the new work, feeling 'quite inspired'. But his unforceful personality made him a less effective conductor than he liked to imagine. The soprano singing the Peri, Livia Fregem, wrote to Clara:

If only you could persuade your dear husband to scold a little, and to insist on greater attention, all would proceed well.

Before their marriage, Robert had promised Clara that one day he would take her to St Petersburg. But when, in 1844, the possibility of such a trip arrived, Robert would have much preferred to stay at home and get on quietly with his writing. Instead, leaving the children with Robert's brother Carl at Schneeburg, they set off in January on a five-month tour. Clara had constantly to remind her husband that the trip had its financial compensations.

Clara played at concerts at Königsberg, Mittau, Riga and Dorpat. They then travelled on to St Petersburg where they met the Tsar. Leaving the capital, they spent Easter at Tver with Robert's uncle, who had settled in Russia. Finally they travelled on to Moscow, where another warm reception awaited them.

The Nevski Prospect, St
Petersburg

The visit did not mean that Schumann became a great deal more familiar with Russian music; he met neither of his Russian contemporaries, Glinka or Alexandre Dargomizshky. He did go to hear Glinka's *A Life for the Tsar* at the opera, but much of it failed to impress him. On the other hand, the sight of the Kremlin inspired Robert to break into verse.

By May Robert and Clara were back in Leipzig. Throughout the tour, Robert had suffered periodic bouts of depression. Whenever he travelled with Clara he felt himself inferior to her, and the further he travelled the more composing-time he felt he was squandering. Ever since November he had been keen to work on an opera, and he had even taken the second part of Goethe's *Faust* with him on the Russian trip, selecting scenes and sketching music when he could snatch the time.

It was becoming increasingly clear that Robert was under considerable stress. He finally decided to resign as editor of the *Zeitschrift*. For ten years the journal had prospered under his guidance, and he now handed over to the new editor, Oswald Lorenz, what he knew was a flourishing concern.

Pursuing his interest in opera, Robert now started work again on *Faust*, but almost immediately switched to setting Byron's *Corsair*. Then he changed his plans again, taking up Hans Christian Andersen's *Lykkens Kalosker*, which he believed he could use for a 'fine magic opera'.

But in August Robert suffered another breakdown. Listening to music became impossible – 'it cut into my nerves as if with knives'. A brief trip to the Harz mountains failed to achieve any improvement. Clara and Robert decided that a complete change was called for, and on 3 October they travelled to Dresden. For the first week or so things were worse rather than better. Robert now had walking problems, could not sleep, and was experiencing hallucinations. Every morning Clara found him 'swimming in tears'.

Clara called in a Dresden physician, a Dr Helbig, who found Robert obsessed with a fear of death and of tall buildings. He also diagnosed a fear of infection, headaches and shivering. Dr Helbig found Schumann a troublesome patient:

As he studied every prescription until he found some reason for not taking it, I ordered him cold plunge baths, which so improved his health that he was able to go back to his usual activity, composing. As I had studied similar cases, especially among men who worked excessively hard at one thing (for instance, accountancy etc.) I advised him to turn his mind to something different from music. He first selected natural history, then natural philosophy, but abandoned them after a few days and gave himself up, wherever he might be, to his musical thoughts.

Robert gradually got better, but had by now decided to leave Leipzig. In October Robert and Clara took an apartment in Dresden's *Waisenhausstrasse*, and in December finally left Leipzig for good. By this time, Mendelssohn had left too, and the Schumanns had few regrets about leaving the city.

7 Dresden

At first Robert Schumann was pleased that music played a relatively insignificant part in Dresden life. 'Here one can get back to the old lost longing for music, there's so little to hear.' But such a novelty did not appeal for long. Dresden was practically dead in musical terms, and such artistic life as existed revolved around the court, consisting of amateur dilettantism and stiff protocol.

When the Schumanns arrived, the only musician to help them was Ferdinand Hiller. Soon he and Robert were attempting to enliven Dresden's musical life with a series of subscription concerts; but progress was painfully slow. Schumann wrote to his friend Mendelssohn:

Dresden, as seen from the right bank of the River Elbe

Ferdinand Hiller
(1811-85)

Richard Wagner in 1842; lithographed portrait by Ernst Kietz

There is nothing to be done with the orchestra; and nothing without it. Convention is all-powerful here. So the band will never play a Beethoven symphony at an extra concert for fear of harming the concert on Palm Sunday and the pension fund.

By coincidence another volatile musician was at work in Dresden at the same time. Richard Wagner was Kapellmeister at the court theatre, and though only thirty-two, was already proving a difficult

Felix Mendelssohn

Johann Sebastian Bach

man to deal with. Incompatible by temperament and ideas, Schumann and Wagner had a troubled relationship. Not surprisingly, Robert did not appreciate the first examples of Wagner's music which he heard. Of *Tannhäuser* he wrote to Mendelssohn:

What does the world (including many musicians) know of pure harmony? There's Wagner, who has just completed another opera, undoubtedly a clever chap, full of mad ideas and bold as you like. The aristocrats are crazy about Rienzi; but I say he cannot write or even imagine four

88

consecutive bars that are melodious – or even right. That's what they all lack – harmony and an ability to write four-part choral stuff.

But when in November 1845 Robert saw *Tannhäuser* on stage, he recognised its dramatic power, and withdrew his former criticism. But he remained suspicious of the methods by which Wagner achieved his ends. For his part, Richard Wagner pronounced Schumann 'too conservative to benefit from my views'.

Rather isolated in Dresden, Robert looked more than ever to Mendelssohn for friendship. He lavished extravagant praise on his work, and wrote in the most affectionate terms:

Well my best love to you. I will write to you again. Indeed, couldn't we write to each other regularly without any special reason? If our friendship was a wine, this would be a vintage year. Perhaps you think the same way, and will write again soon.

Cementing this friendship was a mutual admiration for JS Bach. Sixteen years earlier, Mendelssohn had given the first performances of Bach's *St Matthew Passion* since its composer's lifetime. Now he collaborated with Robert Schumann in arranging for the publication in Berlin of the complete works of Bach. Schumann's enthusiasm for Bach, which grew stronger during 1845, had already resulted in his own new counterpoint compositions. In January he started teaching Clara counterpoint, and in February wrote a fugue for piano. He started an organ fugue based on the letters BACH.

Clara noted this new interest:

Today we began to study counterpoint, which in spite of the labour, gave me great pleasure, for I saw what I had never thought to see – a fugue of my own, and then several more, for we continued our studies regularly every day. Robert himself has been taken with a complete passion for fugues, and beautiful themes pour out of him.

Schumann was also taken with the idea of composing for the pedal-piano, a normal piano with a pedal attachment which allowed the student to practise organ technique. His *Studies and Sketches* were followed by a Rondo for piano and orchestra which was joined to his 1841 *Fantasie* to form his *Piano Concerto in A Minor*. Clara played the first performance of this work in Dresden in December; it is a work which endures as the epitome of romantic youth, with its spring-like brilliance.

But Robert's health was still very precarious. His plans to attend the unveiling of the Beethoven memorial at Bonn in August had to be abandoned. In October he wrote to Mendelssohn:

Wartburg scene from Wagner's *Tannhauser*

Final scene of Act IV from Wagner's *Rienzi*

Schumann's piano room

Unfortunately I haven't recovered my normal strength. Any disturbance of the simple pattern of my existence throws me off balance and into a nervy, irritable state. That is the reason – which I much regret – why I preferred to stay at home when my wife was with you. Whenever there is fun and enjoyment, I keep well away. The only thing is to hope.

Robert experienced once again a block to composing, and turned instead to exercises in counterpoint. Somehow he managed to complete his C major symphony – a weak work – and it was premiered in Leipzig in November 1846. But this year was largely barren, and Robert sank deeper into despair. He toyed with ideas for an opera, but rejected them. In May Clara took Robert to stay with their friend Major Serre at Maxen, but his fears only increased. From the window of his room he could see a lunatic asylum, and he immediately started worrying about his future.

Robert's comfort remained Clara's utter devotion, and his growing family. Two more children had been born since they had

Franz Liszt's private music-room

91

The Karlstheater, Vienna

moved to Dresden: Julie on 11 March 1845, and Emil on 8 February 1846. But when in 1847 Clara realised she was pregnant yet again, she confided in her diary:

What will become of my work? But Robert says: 'Children are a blessing', and he is right. There is no joy without children. I am determined to face the difficult times ahead as cheerfully as I can. Whether I shall always be able to do so, I do not know.

Clara's career did not stagnate completely. In November 1846 she and Robert set off for Vienna to give a series of concerts. But Clara's contempt for virtuoso showpieces had now become well-known, and she selected music by Chopin, Mendelssohn and Schumann himself, for none of which the Viennese had any patience. At the third concert Robert's piano concerto and his Spring Symphony were so coolly received that Clara could no longer conceal her disappointment. Robert tried to point out that 'in ten years' time all this will have changed'. But only the final concert saw any change in their fortunes. By that time, the Schumanns were in the red for the series; but at the last moment Jenny Lind, the Swedish soprano, and a friend of Mendelssohn's, offered to sing with them. She gained a full house for them; but Clara was still unhappy:

I couldn't get over the bitter feeling that one song of Lind's had done what I, with all my playing, could not achieve.

Jenny Lind

93

The couple then went on to Berlin where Robert conducted *Paradise and the Peri* at the *Singakadamie*. The choir was extremely old-fashioned, and had no clue of how to approach contemporary music. On his return to Dresden, Robert once more began looking at various opera projects. He decided on an opera based on Friedrich Hebbel's romantic drama *Genoveva*, which he had just been reading. He finally found himself writing his own libretto and made a start on the overture.

Schumann also returned to *Faust*, and began work on a final chorus. But the death on 22 June of Emil, his youngest child, disrupted the entire household. In July Robert and Clara went back to Zwickau where Schumann was honoured with a music festival featuring a programme entirely composed of his own works. His old music teacher Kuntzsch strutted about 'swelling with pride', and on 10 July Robert conducted a performance of his Second Symphony, together with a chorus specially composed for the event.

But the death of Mendelssohn on 4 November the same year threw Schumann into despondency once again. He went to Leipzig for the memorial service, and upon his return started to write his reminiscences of his friend. Two days after the funeral there was a farewell dinner for Hiller, who was leaving Dresden to take up the post of Director of Music at Düsseldorf. Robert Schumann was now appointed his successor as the conductor of the Dresden men's choir.

This led in turn to Schumann forming a choir for mixed voices, which met for the first time in 1848. He enjoyed his work with this group:

My choral society is a great joy to me. It is made up of sixty or seventy members, and allows me to arrange and adapt any sort of music I choose, according to my own whim . . . On the other hand, I have abandoned the men's chorus. I found insufficient genuine musicianship, and didn't feel up to it, nice fellows though they were.

The choral society sang Bach, Handel and Palestrina, Mendelssohn, Hiller and Schumann's own *Paradise and the Peri*. But Schumann had to face frequent criticism for weakness as a conductor, though one choir member painted a different picture:

True, he had neither the commanding voice nor the commanding eye that forces instant obedience. His voice was a soft, pleasing tenor: his movements quiet. But his whole person displayed the noble nature of a great artist. He had the stamp of genius, and unconsciously raised the entire choir to a high level of intelligence. Everyone felt this to be a matter of serious artistic effort, and that each had to do his best for the good of the choir.

CONVERSAZIONE AND CONCERT OF THE VOCAL ASSOCIATION AT ST. JAMES'S HALL—SEE PRECEDING PAGE.

A nineteenth-century
choral concert

By August 1848 Robert had completed his opera *Genoveva*. He now began work on a project based on Byron's *Manfred*, and was also busy with a piano collection—*Album für die Jugend*:

I wrote the first piece as a birthday gift for my eldest daughter and added the rest at intervals. It seemed I was once again starting out as a composer. You will even find traces of my old humour appearing here and there.

In December he started yet another piano work—*Waldszenen*—a series of pictures reflecting a romantic love of woodland and forest, each piece originally headed by a poetic quotation. One example ran:

The flowers that grow so high are here as pale as death. Only in the middle grows one which gets its dark red not from the sun's glow but from the earth which drank human blood.

After a busy period of composing early in 1849, there came a dramatic interruption. In May, returning to the city from a day in the countryside, the Schumanns arrived to find alarms ringing and shots being fired as Dresden erupted in revolutionary turmoil. The following day the democrats formed a provisional government and barricades (some designed by Richard Wagner) were thrown up. (Wagner was finally forced to flee to Paris, to continue revolutionary pamphleteering from a safe distance.)

Robert Schumann's liberal sentiments were well-known, and he was anxious to avoid being pressed into the militia. When guards called at his house, Robert fled through the back-garden with Clara and Marie, leaving the rest of the children behind. They caught a train to Mügeln, walked to Dohna, and finally found sanctuary with their friend Major Serre at Maxen.

The Dresden uprising. A barricade in the Grosse Frauen Strasse

Devastation in Dresden
following the 1849
uprising

On arriving, Robert's first act was to sit down and write a song.
Clara departed to collect the children who they had left sleeping.
With two other women, and in an advanced state of pregnancy,
Clara set off at three in the morning, braving gunfire and street
battles. She managed to return with all the children safe and
unharmed; Clara noted (presumably without irony) 'my poor
Robert had also spent anxious hours'.

Within a few days the Prussian guards had been called in and the
insurrection suppressed. But Robert was persuaded to wait while
Clara returned once more to Dresden to collect their belongings for
a longer stay in the country. Robert later joined her and they
walked through the streets of Dresden littered with debris, and
'swarming with Prussians'. The next morning the whole family
moved to the little village of Kreischa, where they stayed until mid-
June.

Even these disruptions did not damp Robert's renewed creativity.
Arriving at Kreischa, he first finished off the new *Liederalbum für
die Jugend*. Once more, ideas were were flowing freely, and he
seemed oblivious of outer stress. Shortly before the uprising, he had
written to his friend Hiller:

98

The Schumann children (Julie is missing)

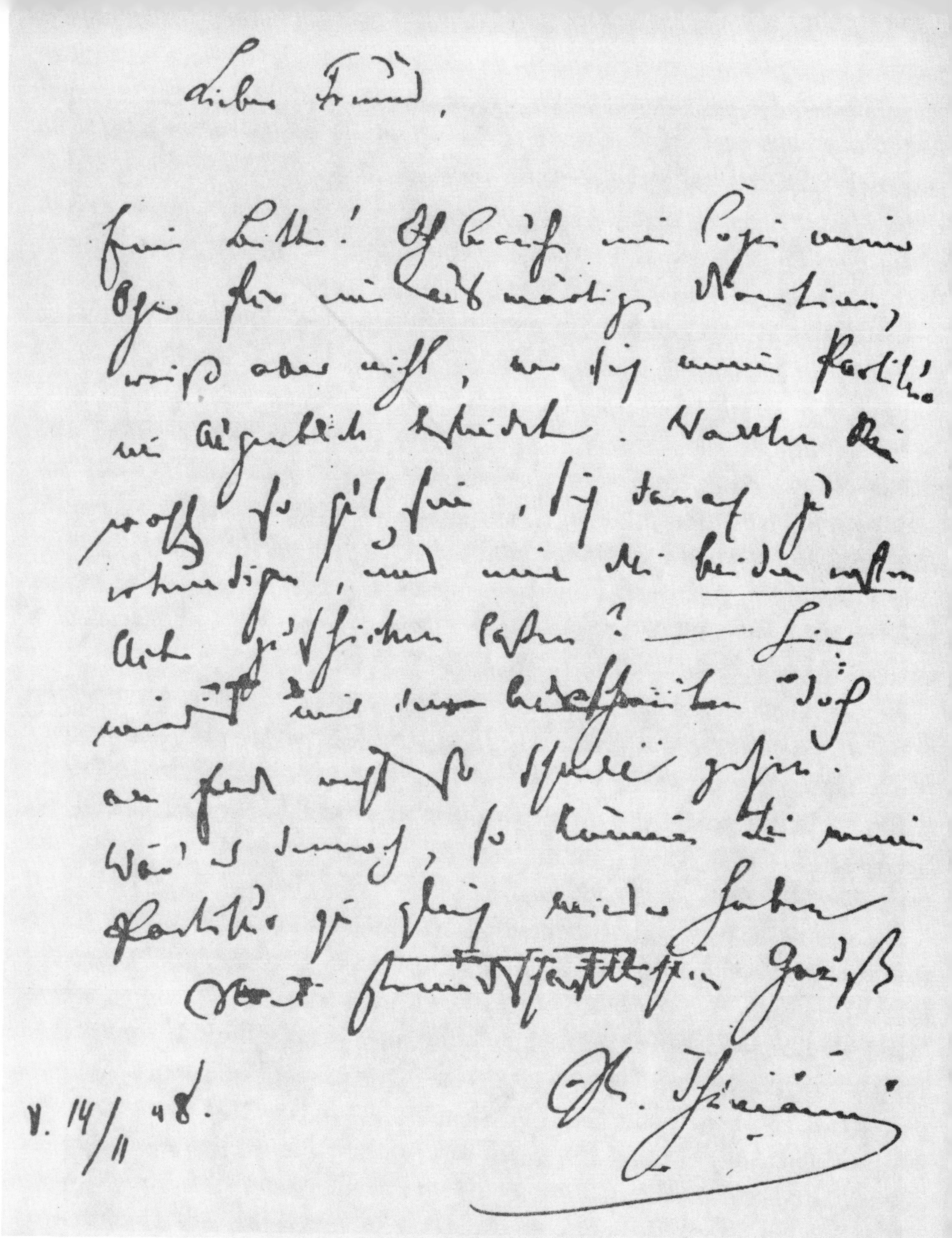

Letter written by Robert Schumann in 1848

I've been busy all this time; it has been my most fruitful year. If is just as though outer storms drive me more into myself, for only in my work do I find any compensation for the terrible storm that burst on me from outside.

Clara was amazed:

It seems to me extraordinary how the terrible happenings outside have awakened his poetic feelings in so completely opposite a way. All his songs breathe a spirit of complete peace. They seem like spring, and laugh like blossoming flowers.

About this time, too, Schumann wrote to Liszt:

We are living very quietly here, and although the great events of the world occupy one's thoughts, my delight in work grows rather than diminishes.

But Robert did echo something of the uprising. He wrote several 'barricade marches', which he eventually sent to a publisher, boldly declaring their sympathies to be republican, and suggesting that the music, written 'with real fiery enthusiasm' should be published at once, with a huge '1849' on the title page. After further thought, he decided to omit this evidence of his revolutionary enthusiasm.

Meanwhile he also set some of Mignon's songs from Goethe's *Faust*, and worked on a *Requiem for Mignon*. He was newly interested in Goethe, and on 29 August, Goethe's birthday, the *Faust* music was performed in the public gardens in Dresden, in Leipzig, and in Goethe's birthplace, Weimar.

Robert had expressed fears about trying to set the verse of so great a writer as Goethe. When some of the Dresden audience told him that his music enhanced their understanding of the literary masterpiece, Schumann was delighted.

But he was irritated by the continuing delays in getting his opera *Genoveva* staged in Leipzig. In the end he had to wait over a year for its first performance. It was finally premiered in June 1850, but after all the waiting did not attract the praise for which Schumann had been hoping.

Robert was now faced with a serious decision. After five years in Dresden, he had made little headway except as a composer. His journalism had more or less dried up, and enquiries about the vacant post of director of the Vienna Conservatoire came to nothing.

Robert received a suggestion from his friend Hiller that he should take over from him as music director at Düsseldorf. However, remembering Mendelssohn's low opinion of Düsseldorf musicians – 'Not a single player in the orchestra can play in tune for

Notre Dame, Dresden

more than a few bars at a time' – Robert delayed his decision. In fact, what alarmed him about Düsseldorf was its lunatic asylum:

The other day I looked for some information about Düsseldorf in an old geography book, and among the places mentioned I discovered three convents and a madhouse. I have no objection to the former, but the latter made me feel anxious. I have to guard myself carefully against any depressing feelings like that. When the sadness of life comes in front of us in all its bare ugliness, it hurts us all the more. At least, that's true with me, with all my fevered imagination.

Clara, however, had no doubts. She disliked Dresden's narrowmindedness. For her such a move was only to the good.

8 Düsseldorf

Whatever his reservations about Düsseldorf, there was no doubting the warm welcome that greeted the Schumanns when they finally arrived there in 1850. They discovered their hotel room to have been filled with flowers. Hiller appeared with the choral society to serenade them. Two days later the local orchestra played Mozart's *Don Giovanni* overture as they sat down for dinner. Finally a dinner and ball were arranged in their honour. Schumann was welcomed with a fanfare and a concert of his own compositions. But the couple were exhausted, and left before the ball even began. They also had to miss an excursion that Hiller organised the next day.

Since student days, Schumann had adored the Rhineland. To be actually living on the great river meant much to him. Clara had the possibility of new opportunities there, and Robert, with a choir and an orchestra at his disposal, enjoyed enviable resources as a composer. The musicians had been well trained by Mendelssohn, Rietz and Hiller, and Schumann's duties as a conductor were light enough not to interrupt his work as a composer. A suitable home was finally located for the Schumann family, and Robert felt his confidence increase.

Düsseldorf

In September Robert and Clara visited Cologne, and were enormously impressed by the soaring medieval cathedral. It was during this visit that Robert seems to have been stimulated to produce the ideas later expressed in the slow movement of his third symphony, the 'Rhenish'.

In October Robert turned his attention to a cello concerto, and the day he completed it conducted the first subscription concert of the season. Robert was pleased with the standard of the orchestra, and in the season which followed, conducted first performances of several of his works, including the *Requiem for Mignon*, the *Neujahrslied*, the *Rhenish Symphony*, the *Nachlied* for chorus and orchestra, and an overture to Schiller's *Braut von Messina*.

By March 1851 Robert felt fitter than at any time since arriving in Düsseldorf. But in that month an anonymous article attacking his direction of the season's concerts appeared in the *Düsseldorfer Zeitung*. As a conductor, he was always retiring, and sometimes positively vague, and a concert on 13 March had been well below standard. The attack upset Robert, and a few days later he wrote in his diary: 'doubts about staying longer at Düsseldorf'. Only a successful performance of Bach's *St John Passion* seems to have brought a temporary halt to the criticism.

Cologne Cathedral

103

In April Moritz Horn sent Robert a sentimental poem, *Der Rose Pilgerfahrt*, about a rose that turns into a princess. He set it for solo voices, chorus and piano. In June he returned to a set of piano duets, later published as *Ball-szenen*. Schumann also discussed with the Elberfeld publisher, FW Arnold, collecting about thirty piano pieces under the title 'Chaff' (*Spreu*). In the end fourteen of them were published, under the new title 'Coloured Pages' (*Bunter Blätter*). The original idea was to issue each on a different coloured paper, but this idea was dropped.

In July *Der Rose Pilgerfahrt* was given a successful private performance in the Schumanns' drawing-room by a small group of singers. From this group Robert formed a chamber choir which met fortnightly in different members' homes to sing Bach motets and music by such composers as Lassus and Palestrina.

Robert and Clara now took a long summer holiday, travelling up the Rhine to Heidelberg. From there they went on to Baden-Baden, Basel, Geneva, Chamonix and Vevey. On their return to Düsseldorf in August, they received a visit from Liszt and his mistress, the Princess Carolyn Sayn-Wittgenstein.

But on returning home, Schumann met an unpleasant shock. Most of the Düsseldorf choir was made up of enthusiastic amateurs, who were increasingly puzzled by Schumann's uncommunicative methods. At one rehearsal the sopranos stopped singing when they went wrong. Soon the rest of the choir followed suit, but Schumann, immersed in the music, failed to notice, and went on conducting regardless. Julius Tausch, the accompanist, and

A nineteenth-century male-voice choir

assistant to Schumann, eventually stopped too. But when Schuman beckoned him to the dais, it was not to complain, but to point to the score: 'Look, this bar is beautiful!'

Schumann was becoming lethargic and incompetent as a musician. In August there was a meeting of the choir when Robert launched into an outburst. Members started to stay away, performances deteriorated. Schumann had a quarrel with the assistant burgomaster, who was also secretary of the choir. Robert once more speculated about his future in Düsseldorf, and told a

Robert and Clara
Schumann

friend he was 'very angry with certain people'. Composing remained Robert's solace. He continually orchestrated, arranged and composed. Since 1846, Schumann had been wondering about working on a 'concert oratorio' based on Goethe's romantic drama *Hermann und Dorothea*. He now wrote a very poor overture for it.

In 1852 Robert was busy preparing the choir to perform parts of Bach's *B Minor Mass* and the *St Matthew Passion*, marking a new interest in spiritual music. He had once said 'If a man knows the Bible, Shakespeare and Goethe, and has taken them to himself, he needs nothing more'. He had written with similar sentiments to a Dutch singer named Strackerjan in 1852:

It must always be the artist's highest aim to direct his efforts towards sacred music. In youth we are so firmly rooted to the earth with its joys and sorrows, though as we get older our branches aspire to greater things. I hope this will be true of me before long.

Schumann began work at this time on a setting of the mass and a requiem. He was also busy with some of his old articles, with the idea of publishing them in book-form. This turned out to be more difficult than he envisaged, and he had to try two publishers in vain before finding a home for his manuscript with George Wigand. In 1852 Robert's health took a turn for the worse. In April he suffered a form of paralytic attack, which was accompanied by sleeplessness and depression. By June he was worse still, and could not go to Weimar to hear a performance of his incidental music to *Manfred*. Many of his old symptoms returned, together with an alarming new speech impediment.

A trip to Godesberg at the end of June to find a cure only made him worse. His doctor prescribed sea bathing, and Clara went with him to Scheveningen. But when he arrived back in Düsseldorf he was warned to avoid excessive exertions. In October he suffered severe giddy attacks, while November brought 'remarkable aural symptoms'. He had to ask Tausch to conduct the first two concerts of the season. Gossip bred.

Finally Schumann re-appeared to conduct on 3 December. The performance was badly received; the choir had been much happier working under the efficient Tausch. Three committee members requested Schumann's resignation. After stormy sessions, they were forced to withdraw and to apologise. But the damage had been done, and Schumann's confidence severely jolted. Tacit agreement was reached that Tausch should train the choir, and Schumann restrict himself to orchestra rehearsals and public concerts.

The 1853 Lower Rhine Festival was quite successful. Schumann's Fourth Symphony received its premiere on the opening day, but his friend Hiller undertook the major burden of conducting. The papers certainly preferred his work.

Manuscript of Bach's *St. Matthew Passion*

The Beethoven monument in Bonn

Meanwhile Robert's friends were becoming more and more concerned about his health. He had developed a morbid interest in table-rapping and the occult, and even wrote an article about it. He wrote to Hiller:

'Yesterday we had table-turning for the first time. A wonderful power! Just fancy, I asked what was the rhythm of the first two bars of the C minor symphony. There was more hesitation than normal about the answer. At last it came . . . rather slowly at first, but when I said, 'But the tempo ought to be rather faster, dear table!' it was promptly rapped out in the right time. I also asked whether it could tell the number I had thought of, and it gave three absolutely correctly. We were all lost in amazement and felt surrounded by miracles . . .

In July, during a visit to Bonn, Schumann apparently suffered a slight stroke. A doctor was called after a seizure. But the music still poured forth – piano reductions, orchestral arrangements, piano pieces. A fantasy for violin and orchestra, and a violin concerto were both written for the twenty-two-year-old Joachim, protegé of Mendelssohn's at Leipzig, whose playing of the Beethoven concerto at the Lower Rhine Festival in May greatly impressed Schumann. In August Joachim visited Düsseldorf and delighted Robert with his virtuosity.

It was Joachim who brought the twenty-year-old Johannes Brahms to the Schumanns' home late in September 1853. Robert's daughter Marie remembered the occasion well:

One day . . . towards noon the doorbell rang, and I rushed, as children do, to open the door. A very young man, beautiful as the day, with long fair hair, stood in front of me. He asked for my father, and I answered that both my parents were out. Then he asked when he could come back, and I said tomorrow at eleven, for my parents generally went out at twelve. The next day he came back at eleven. (We were at school.) My father asked him in. He had brought his compositions and my father thought that, as he was there, the best thing was for him to play them himself. The young man sat down at the piano. But after the first few bars, my father interrupted him saying 'Please wait a moment; I must fetch my wife . . .' Dinner that day is engraved upon my memory. Both my parents were enchanted and deeply moved, and could not stop talking about the genius who had visited them that morning, Johannes Brahms.

Johannes Brahms at the age of twenty, in 1853, by JB Laurens. Pencil drawing done at Düsseldorf on the request of Robert Schumann

Brahms and Joachim

Brahms' manuscript of his first sonata, Op. 1

Robert recognised immediately the genius in the rather gauche young composer. Two early piano sonatas and a scherzo were enough to persuade him of Brahms' potential. After nine years' silence, Robert contributed the famous 'New Ways' article to the *Neue Zeitschrift:* 'to assist the young eagle in his first flight through the world'.

On 27 October Joachim arrived in Düsseldorf to give the first performance of Schumann's Fantasy at the opening concert of the new season. Meanwhile Robert started work on a cooperative venture, a violin sonata based on the initials of Joachim's romantic motto '*Frei aber Einsame*' (free but alone). Working with Brahms and the young composer Albert Dietrich, Robert Schumann wrote the second and fourth movements. The work completed, Joachim played it to Clara's piano accompaniment. Immediately afterwards Schumann started work on new movements to replace those of Brahms and Dietrich; the result was his third violin sonata.

Now the storm over Schumann's role in Düsseldorf musical life finally burst. The concert on 27 October 1853 was to be the last Robert ever conducted in Düsseldorf. Following a disastrous performance a fortnight earlier, the choir refused to sing under Schumann's baton. Tausch took over, but a rehearsal directed by Schumann on the day of the concert fell into chaos. Ever since the spring, the orchestra had been discovering that Robert wanted them to play slower and slower. Sometimes he stood at his dais, arms raised to conduct, but not moving. Tiring of delay, the orchestra often started without him. Sometimes he rehearsed the same passage time and time again, without explaining why. Once he stopped the trombonist, telling him he had missed a cue. The passage was repeated, and Robert said: 'It's alright now. It sounds good'. In fact the player had not played a note.

Soon patience was running out. Clara saw the next series of events as intriguing by Tausch, but Schumann's deputy was in fact devoted to his sick superior. On 7 November the chairman and another committee member requested Schumann to restrict himself to conducting his own music, leaving the rest to Tausch. There was no malice in the committee's moves, and by the end of the year Schumann's incapacity was obvious to all. The city burgomaster attempted to conciliate between the committee and the sick and injured composer, but Robert Schumann never responded.

Robert had one consolation. Towards the end of 1853 he wrote:

My music is spreading more and more, in other countries too, especially in Holland and England, and it always delights the artist to see that – for it is not praise that brings about this rejoicing, but joy that what he has felt in himself finds echoes in peoples' hearts.

In his thinking, Robert was always the complete romantic. When still only twenty-two he wrote:

I believe music to be the ideal language of the soul: some think it is only intended to tickle the ear, while others treat it like a mathematical calculation.

Marriage brought him stability and a deep contentment. Only his broken health sapped his confidence, so that with age he increasingly withdrew into himself, striving to maintain his routine, and to avoid travel, trivial conversation and similar distractions. For Clara's sake he made himself accept a number of appointments which forced him into the public eye – but which he palpably failed to carry out as satisfactorily as if he had been fit.

Robert Schumann, by H. Best

9 Twilight

Early in 1854 Robert and Clara visited Hanover. They heard Joachim play his fantasy. Clara played on two occasions at court, and spent much time with Brahms. Arriving back home, Robert continued work on a poetry anthology he had started. He went to the municipal library to research it, to the alarm of Clara, who could see the strain her husband was suffering from. In February Robert wrote to Joachim:

Meanwhile, I have been working at my garden which is growing more and more imposing. I have added some sign posts to keep people from staring – i.e. an explanatory text. I am at the moment occupied with the ancients – Homer and the Greeks. In Plato particularly I have discovered some wonderful passages.

But at the beginning of the letter there is a clear indication of Robert's mental state:

We have been away a whole week without sending you or your companions a sign. But I have often written to you in spirit and there is invisible writing, which will appear later, underlying this. I will close now. It is growing dark . . .

Darkness fell on the night of 10 February. A solitary note now beat in Robert's ears, giving him no peace. He called it 'a very strong and painful' experience. Now there came music 'more wonderful and played by more exquisite instruments than ever sounded on earth'. On the seventeenth he leapt out of bed to scribble down a theme which he claimed the angels had given him. The pattern of notes was very similar to those in the slow movement of his violin concerto, finished the previous autumn. The angels now turned to demons, tigers and hyenas which taunted him with damnation.

Clara described Robert's hearing delusions:

My poor Robert suffers terribly. All sounds are transformed for him into music . . . He has said several times that if it does not stop he'll go out of his mind . . . The trouble with his ears has now got to the point of his hearing great symphonic pieces played right through with the last note held on until another piece comes into his mind.

Clara Schumann

113

On 26 February Robert begged Clara to have him committed to an asylum, but was finally persuaded by the doctor to go to bed. Clara recorded in her diary the events that followed:

Robert got up, but was more wretched than words can say. If I even touched him, he said 'Ah! Clara, I am not worthy of your love'. He said this, the one to whom I always look up with the greatest, the deepest reverence, and nothing I could say was of any use. He made a fair copy of the *Variations*, and when he got to the end suddenly left the room and

Joseph Joachim
(1831-1907)

114

went sighing to his bedroom. I had left the room for only a few minutes, to say something to Dr Hasenclever, and had left little Marie sitting with him (for ten days I had never left him alone for a minute). Marie thought he would come back in a minute, but he didn't. He ran out into the most frightful rain wearing nothing but his coat – no boots or waistcoat.

Bertha suddenly burst in, telling me he had gone. No words can describe my emotions. I felt as though my heart stopped beating. Dietrich, Hasenclever, indeed everyone there, ran out to find him – but with no success. An hour later two strangers brought him back. Where and how they found him I could not find out.

Only later did she discover that Robert had thrown himself into the River Rhine, and fishermen had rescued him.

On 4 March Robert was taken to Dr Richarz's private asylum at Endenich, near Bonn. At intervals his mind cleared a little. In August, for instance, he said he wanted to receive a letter from Clara, who was not permitted to see him. He was sane enough to reply rationally, and for the next seven months sustained a quite normal correspondence with her, asking her about the children, her playing, his manuscripts and other matters.

On Christmas Eve 1854 Robert received a visit from Joachim, and 11 January 1855 was considered fit enough to see Brahms. In March he even did some new work on a piano accompaniment. However another visit from Brahms resulted in a serious relapse, and on 5 May he wrote to Clara for the last time. A visitor listening

The Rhine at Cologne

Clara Schumann, a pencil
drawing by Lehmann

to Robert playing the piano at his asylum in the summer described it as like 'a machine whose springs are broken, but which still tries to work, jerking convulsively'.

On 10 September 1855 Dr Richarz informed Clara that he could offer no hope of Robert's recovery. He was incurably insane. Now he suffered disorders of taste and smell, and ever deeper depression.

There has been much discussion about the nature of Schumann's illness. Recently doctors have suggested, on the evidence of Dr Richarz' autopsy and the symptoms of the last twelve years of his life, that he died of syphilitic disease – 'a combination of cerebrospinal syphilis and *dementia paralytica*'. Such a diagnosis accounts for his physical convulsions and partial paralysis, and for his mental delusions concerning strange sounds and giddiness. It is likely that he contracted the disease during his promiscuous years as a student.

But Robert's health improved periodically during his time at Endenich. In September 1854 he could write quite rationally to Clara:

What joyful tidings you have again sent me! The birth of a fine boy – and in June, too; the way in which the dear girls, Marie and Elise, celebrated your birthday by playing you the *Bilder aus Osten* to your own surprise and mine; Brahms' removal to Düsseldorf for good (please give him my kindest remembrances) – these are indeed happy tidings! . . . I was pleased to hear that a complete collection of my writings, the concerto for cello, the violin fantasie (which Joachim plays so splendidly) and the *Fughetten* had been published. Can you, since you offer so lovingly, send me any of these? Please remember me to Joachim when you write to him. What have Brahms and Joachim been composing? . . . You say that you give lessons in the music room. What pupils have you now? And which are the best? Don't you find it tiring, dearest Clara?

8pm. I have just got back from Bonn, where I paid my regular visit to Beethoven's statue, which always delights me. As I was standing in front of it, the organ in the cathedral church started playing. I am much stronger again, and look younger than when I was in Düsseldorf. Now I have a request to make. Will you write and ask Dr Peters to give me some money from time to time, when I want it, and let you pay it back to him? It makes me so sad to have nothing to give to a beggar. My life is less eventful than it used to be. How different everything was then.

On 8 June 1856, Robert's birthday, Brahms found him thin, oblivious of everything outside, picking names out of an atlas and putting them into alphabetical order. On 23 July Clara was informed by telegram that he was nearing the end. She hurried to Endenich, but the crisis passed. She was summoned again on 27 July, and actually saw Robert for the first time for over two years. He seemed to recognise his wife, but could not form any words to speak. Clara recalled these last hours:

I saw him between six and seven in the evening. He smiled and put his arm around me with enormous effort, for he cannot now control his limbs. I shall never forget it.

Not all the treasure of this world could equal his embrace. My Robert; in such a way we saw each other again. How bitter it was to trace your dear features! What a tragic sight.

Two-and-a-half years ago you were dragged from me with no farewell, though your heart must have been full. Now I lay at your feet, hardly daring to breathe, and just now and then glimpsing a look, clouded, but unutterably gentle.

Johannes Brahms

On Thursday 29 July Robert was finally released from his suffering. At four in the afternoon he fell asleep. He passed away without anyone noticing. Clara did not see him till half an hour later.

His head was beautiful, the forehead so transparent and slightly arched. I stood by the body of my beloved husband, and I was at peace. All my

Bonn Cathedral

119

Clara Schumann

feelings were taken up in thanks to God that Robert was at last free, and as I knelt by his bed I was filled with awe. It was as though his sacred spirit was hovering above me. If only he had taken me with him.

Schumann was buried at seven o'clock on the morning of 31 July 1856 in Bonn. Brahms and Joachim walked in front of the coffin, which was carried by some of the Düsseldorf choir. Clara asked that few friends be there:

His dearest friends walked in front, and I came unnoticed behind. It was best this way. He would have liked it so. So, with his departure, my happiness is ended. A new life is beginning.

One writer sums up the tragedy of Schumann's last years:

The terror of his last years was that he, who had lived for feeling and communion with the beloved, was caged in the silence of his solitude. Feeling was followed by inertia; the dreams of his youth

Bonn

121

became hallucinations. Schubert dictated to him sublime themes which he could not, alas, remember; the obsessive rhythms which had pounded through his youth became a single pounded note reiterated in his head – sound and fury, now signifying nothing . . . Schumann now came to live in a past which he could no longer believe in; in the dream of his madness, the dreams he had lived for seemed a sham. His music, if sometimes almost unbearably poignant, is never tragic; but in contemplating the romantic myth which is his life one certainly feels both pity and terror. It is difficult to imagine anything more appalling than the letter which he wrote to Clara from the asylum, asking her to send him the little tune he had written for her 'long ago, when we were in love'. He was forty-two.

Memorial to Schumann

122

A Schumann Chronology

1810   8 June Robert Schumann born at Zwickau

1816   Placed at private school

1820   Starts at Lyceum, Zwickau

1826   Emilie, Robert's sister, commits suicide. His father, August Schumann, dies

1828   Leaves Lyceum, tours Bavaria with Rosen. Enters Leipzig University to study law. Takes music lessons with Wieck, and meets his daughter Clara

1829   Enrols at Heidelberg University to study law under Thibaut. Vacation in Italy

1830   Returns to Leipzig to devote himself to music. First symptoms of injury to hand

1831   Completes *Papillons*

1832   Hand injury makes him give up piano

1833   Julius, Robert's brother, dies. Falls in love with Ernestine

1834   Launches *Neue Zeitschrift für Musik*

1835   Completes *Carnaval* and *Piano Sonata no 1*

1836   Mother dies. Falls in love with Clara Wieck; beginning of struggle with her father

1837   Engaged to Clara. Writes *Davidsbündlertänze*

1838   Visits Vienna and discovers ms of Schubert's *'Great' Symphony*. Writes *Kinderscenen* and *Kreisleriana*

1839   Appeals to court to marry Clara. Wieck accuses him of drunkenness. Death of Eduard, his eldest brother

1840   Marries Clara. His 'song year': *Liederkreis, Myrthen, Frauenliebe und -leben*

1841   Finishes *Spring Symphony*. Daughter Marie born

1842   'Chamber-music year'

1843   Wieck tries to mend quarrel. Elise Schumann born

1844   Tour to Berlin, Könisberg and Russia. Gives up editing *Neue Zeitschrift für Musik*. Nervous breakdown

1845   Settles in Dresden. *A minor piano concerto*. Julie Schumann born

1846   Health worsens; constant roaring in ears

1847   Summer festival for Schumann at Zwickau

1848   Ludwig Schumann born

1849   Leaves Dresden because of uprising. His 'most fruitful period'. Ferdinand Schumann born

1850 Concert tour of Germany. Move to Düsseldorf. *Cello concerto*
1851 Difficulties as conductor of Düsseldorf orchestra
1852 Quarrels over orchestra
1853 Meets and recognises Brahms
1854 Plagued by imaginary sounds. Attempts suicide. Taken to private asylum at Endenich
1855 Brahms befriends Clara
1856 Dies 29 July

Autograph of Clara Schumann

Painting depicting the "romantic" Schumann

The Complete Works of Robert Schumann

KEYBOARD MUSIC

SOLO PIANO

Op No, Title, Date of Composition

1   Theme on the name ABEGG with Variations, 1830
2   Papillons, 1829-31
3   6 Studies on Paganini Caprices, 1832
4   6 Intermezzi, 1832
5   Impromptus on a theme by Clara Wieck, 1833
6   Davidsbündlertänze: 18 Characteristic Pieces, 1837
7   Toccata in C ma, 1831
8   Allegro in B mi, 1831
9   Carnaval: Scènes mignonnes sur quatres notes, 1834-5
     1   Préambule
     2   Pierrot
     3   Arlequin
     4   Valse Noble
     5   Eusebius
     6   Florestan
     7   Coquette
     8   Réplique
     9   Sphinxes
     10   Papillons
     11   ASCH-SCHA
     12   Chiarina
     13   Chopin
     14   Estrella
     15   Reconnaissance
     16   Pantalon et Colombine
     17   Valse allemande
     18   Paganini
     19   Aveu
     20   Promenade
     21   Pause
     22   Marche des 'Davidsbündler' contre les Philistins
10   6 Concert Studies on Paganini Caprices (Set II), 1833
11   Sonata No 1, F sharp mi, 1833-5

12	Fantasiestücke, 1837
	1 Des Abends
	2 Aufschwung
	3 Warum?
	4 Grillen
	5 In der Nacht
	6 Fabel
	7 Traumes Wirren
	8 Ende vom Lied
	9 ★ ★ ★
13	Etudes en forme de variations, 1834-7
14	Sonata No 3, F mi, 1835-6
15	Kinderscenen, 1838
	1 Vom fremden Ländern und Menschen
	2 Curiose Geschichte
	3 Hasche-Mann
	4 Bittendes Kind
	5 Glückes genug
	6 Wichtige Begebenheit
	7 Traümerei
	8 Am Camin
	9 Ritter vom Steckenpferd
	10 Fast zu ernst
	11 Fürchtenmachen
	12 Kind im Einschlummern
	13 Der Dichter spricht
16	Kreisleriana – 8 fantasies, 1838
17	Fantasie in C ma, 1836
18	Arabeske in C ma, 1839
19	Blumenstück in Db ma, 1839
20	Humoreske in Bb ma, 1838
21	Novelleten, 1838
22	Sonata No 2, G mi, 1833-8
23	4 Nachtstücke, 1839
26	Faschingsschwank aus Wien, 1839
	1 Allegro
	2 Romanze
	3 Scherzino
	4 Intermezzo
	5 Finale
28	3 Romanzen, 1839
	1 Bb mi
	2 F sharp ma
	3 B ma
32	Clavierstücke, 1838-9
	1 Scherzo in Bb ma

    2 Leides Ahnung
    3 Scherzino
    4 Walzer
    5 Fantasiestanz
    6 Wiegenliedchen
    7 Ländler
    8 Lied ohne Ende
    9 Impromptu
   10 Walzer
   11 Romanze
   12 Burla
   13 Larghetto
   14 Vision
   15 Walzer
   16 Schlummerlied
   17 Elfe
   18 Botschaft
   19 Fantasiestück
   20 Canon
126 Sieben Clavierstücke in Fughettenform, 1853
    1 A mi
    2 D mi
    3 F ma
    4 D mi
    5 A mi
    6 F ma
    7 A mi
133 Gesänge der Frühe, 1853
    1 D ma
    2 D ma
    3 A ma
    4 F sharp mi
    5 D ma

In addition a number of unfinished, unpublished, or un-numbered
works.

PIANO DUETS

    Eight Polonaises, 1828
 66 Bilder aus Osten, 6 Impromptus, 1848
 85 Zwölf vierhändige Clavierstücke für kleine und grosse
    Kinder, 1849
    1 Geburtstagsmarsch
    2 Bärentanz
    3 Gartenmelodi
    4 Beim Kränzewinden
    5 Kroatenmarsch

6 Trauer

7 Turniermarsch

8 Reigen

9 Am Springbrunnen

10 Versteckens

11 Gespenstermärchen

12 Abendlied

109 Ballscenen, 1851

    1 Préambule

    2 Polonaise

    3 Walzer

    4 Ungarisch

    5 Française

    6 Mazurka

    7 Ecossaise

    8 Walzer

    9 Promenade

130 'Kinderball', 1853

    1 Polonaise

    2 Walzer

    3 Menuett

    4 Ecossaise

    5 Française

    6 Ringelreihe

TWO PIANOS

46   Andante and Variations in Bb ma, 1843

PEDAL PIANOFORTE

56   'Studien für den Pedal-Flügel', 1845

58   'Skizzen für den Pedal-Flügel', 1845

ORGAN

60   'Six Fugues on the name of BACH', 1845

HARMONIUM

Piece in two movements, F ma

SONGS

24   Liederkreis Vol I, 1840

    1 Morgens steh' ich auf

    2 Es Treibt mich hin

    3 Ich wandelte unter den Bäumen

    4 Lieb' Liebchen

    5 Schöne Wiege meiner Leiden

    6 Warte, warte, wilder Schiffsman

INSTRUMENTAL CHAMBER MUSIC

Clara Schumann and Joachim playing in concert

The titlepage for Schumann's cycle
Songs for the Young

Kapellmeister Kreisler, whom Schumann immortalized in his
Kreisleriana, a cycle of piano pieces dedicated to Chopin

63 Piano Trio No 1, D mi, 1847

70 Adagio and Allegro in Ab ma for horn and piano, 1849

73 Fantasiestücke for clarinet and piano, 1849

80 Piano Trio No 2, 1847

88 Fantasiestücke, 1842

94 Drei Romanzen for oboe and piano, 1849

102 Fünf Stücke im Volkston for cello and piano, 1849

105 Sonata No 1 in A mi for violin and piano, 1851

110 Piano Trio No 3, 1851

113 Märchenbildern for viola and piano, 1851

121 Sonata No 2 in D mi, violin and piano, 1851

132 Märchenerzälungen for clarinet, violin and piano, 1853

Plus other works unfinished, unpublished or without opus numbers.

VOCAL CHAMBER MUSIC

29 Drei Gedichte, 1840
  1 Ländliches Lied
  2 Lied
  3 Zigeunerleben

34 Vier Duette für Sopran und Tenor, 1840
  1 Liebesgarten
  2 Liebhabers Ständchen
  3 Unter'm Fenster
  4 Familien -Gemälde

43 Drei zweistimmige Lieder, 1840
  1 Wenn ich ein Vöglein wär
  2 Herbstlied
  3 Schön Blümelein

64 Auf ihrem Grab, 1847

74 Spanisches Liederspiel, 1849
  1 Erste Begegnung
  2 Intermezzo
  3 Liebesgram
  4 In der Nacht
  5 Es ist verraten
  6 Melancholie
  7 Geständnis
  8 Botchaft
  9 Ich bin geliebt
  10 Der Contrabandiste

78 Vier Duette für Sopran und Tenor, 1849
  1 Tanzlied
  2 Er und sie
  3 Ich denke dein
  4 Wiegenlied

ORCHESTRAL MUSIC

CONCERTOS, etc

CHORAL MUSIC, WITH ORCHESTRA

CHORAL PARTSONGS

OPERA AND THEATRE MUSIC

Further reading

Gerald Abraham ed *Schumann: A Symposium*, OUP, Oxford, 1954

Thomas A Brown, *The Aesthetics of Robert Schumann*, New York, 1968

Joan Chissell, *Schumann*, Dent, London, 1977

Joan Chissell, *Schumann: The Piano Music*, BBC, London, 1972

Frederick Niecks, *Robert Schumann*, London, 1925

Herbert F Peyser, *Robert Schumann: Tone-poet, Prophet and Critic*, New York, 1948

Eric Sams, *The Songs of Robert Schumann*, Eulenberg, London, 1969

Robert H Schauffler: *Florestan: The Life and Work of Robert Schumann*, New York, 1945

Henry Pleasants ed, *The Musical World of Robert Schumann*, Victor Gollancz, London, 1965

Alan Walker, *Schumann*, Barrie and Jenkins, London, 1976

Alan Walker, *Robert Schumann, The Man and his Music*, Faber, London, 1972

Stephen Walsh, *The Lieder of Schumann*, London, 1971

Percy M Young, *Tragic Muse*, London, 1957

Percy M Young, *Schumann*, London, 1976

Index

Illustrations are indicated in bold type

ILLUSTRATIONS ADDED FOR EXPANDED EDITION

In creating this expanded edition, more than thirty illustrations have been added as unnnumbered pages at various places within the text. Following is a key to those insertions.